ZOE ADJONYOH

Zoe's ghana Kitchen

ZOE ADJONYOH

Zoe's ghana kitchen

Traditional Ghanaian recipes
remixed for the modern kitchen

An Hachette UK Company
www.hachette.co.uk

First published in Great Britain in 2017 by
Mitchell Beazley, a division of Octopus Publishing Group Ltd
Carmelite House, 50 Victoria Embankment, London EC4Y 0DZ
www.octopusbooks.co.uk
www.octopusbooksusa.com

Design and Layout Copyright © Octopus Publishing Group Ltd 2017
Text Copyright © Zoe Adjonyoh 2017

Distributed in the US by Hachette Book Group
1290 Avenue of the Americas, 4th and 5th Floors, New York, NY 10020

Distributed in Canada by Canadian Manda Group
664 Annette St., Toronto, Ontario, Canada M6S 2C8

ISBN 978-1-78472-163-3

A CIP catalogue record for this book is available from the British Library.

Printed and bound in China

10 9 8 7 6 5 4 3 2 1

Editorial Director: Eleanor Maxfield
Editor: Pollyanna Poulter
Art Director: Yasia Williams
Photographer: Nassima Rothacker
Food Stylist: Polly Webb-Wilson
Production Manager: Caroline Alberti

CONTENTS

INTRODUCTION

★ 'Oh! I've never tried that before.' This is the usual response when I mention Ghanaian food and tell people what I do for a living. This is what has inspired me to write this cookbook.

African cuisine has been surprisingly marginalized, both in people's consciousness and on the high street. We don't see African cookery shows on TV; we rarely see reviews of the myriad pan-African restaurants serving up great food from an incredibly rich and diverse continent, whose influences have nevertheless spread all over the world.

I believe we are on the cusp of an African food revolution. Among a generation of foodies whose palates are exhausted by innumerable variations on the burger, there is a longing to try something that is new, not just re-spun. African cuisines are filling that gap. It's the last continent of relatively unexplored food.

Within the African diaspora, two important trends are taking place. First, people are transporting themselves 'back home' to reconnect with the culture of their parents and grandparents, bringing with them their knowledge of and appetite for modern Western business and entrepreneurship in order to resettle, repackage and export what is good about their homelands. But also, being members of that same generation of foodies, they want to show off the vibrancy and variety of their home nation's cuisine wherever they reside.

For too long, Africans have kept their amazing food a greedy secret, cooked and closely guarded by mothers and grandmothers in the home, then rolled out just for celebratory occasions such as weddings and naming ceremonies. Only a select few friends outside of the African community are admitted to the inner sanctum of the African kitchen to sample these delicious morsels.

Very good West African restaurants exist in London and other cities in the West, they really do, yet they are cloistered in the community and there has been no attempt to encourage the crossover of those cuisines into mainstream eating out – until now. This is the main mission behind Zoe's Ghana Kitchen, my cooking and dining venture: to share the passion of and for this food with a wider audience. Suddenly we are seeing a whole new raft of pop-ups and supper clubs representing Nigeria, Sierra Leone, Congo and Togo and I suspect (and hope) we will witness those go on to launch as restaurants in the coming years. And it's not just West Africa being represented – it's a continent-wide food movement that's taking place... and it's incredibly exciting!

It's important to note that I am not a trained chef, nor did I grow up with a Ghanaian grandmother pouring her cooking influence into me. I am self-taught, and that should encourage anyone who is new to Ghanaian food or wants to reconnect with it.

The point of this book is not to give a definitive guide to Ghanaian cuisine but to highlight Ghana's great ingredients, subtle flavour profiles and cooking methods, and – most importantly – to make that food accessible and highlight how to incorporate those ingredients easily into everyday dishes.

Within these pages, I have sought to strike a balance in the recipes between paying homage to traditional cooking methods and styles, and my own interpretations of certain authentic dishes. I've also given some new ways to incorporate favourite Ghanaian ingredients into other dishes, for those already familiar with good home-cooked Ghanaian food.

How to Use this Book

★ I'd love to see more people incorporating West African ingredients and flavours into their everyday life without trepidation. I hope that recipes such as Chunky Yam Chips, Suya Steak Bavette, Jollof Fried Chicken, Savoury Fried Yam and Akara (bean fritters), for example, demonstrate how easy it can be to mix it up a little and bring those flavours into everyday cooking. The spice mixes, too, should encourage people to be adventurous with flavouring and marinating dishes in celebration of Ghanaian food!

You will no doubt be pleasantly surprised by the relative ease of cooking or preparing most of the dishes. Although there are some ingredients that may be hard to come by, they can often be substituted as I have suggested, and where they can't, please refer to the list of stockists (see pages 254–5) – the internet makes it increasingly easy to source these ingredients if you don't have a local African grocer nearby.

That being said, these recipes are not didactic. The methods for most of the traditional dishes have been handed down orally and vary from region to region, and there are innumerable variations up and down Ghana on the ways of cooking and the ingredients used. This makes the recipes super-flexible, as you can take the basic principles and adapt them easily to what you have available in your cupboard or fridge. In any case, recipes that don't adapt over time risk being lost completely.

This book is for anyone with an interest in food and an inquisitive palate, and there should be something for everyone within these pages.

My Food Journey

★ My journey to and exploration of Ghanaian cuisine has been led by a very personal desire to make a connection with an aspect of my ancestry – a people and a culture that were largely distant in my upbringing – and it has been supplemented by the joy of bringing folk together over food.

Though I spent my early years in Accra, being weaned on 'Tom Brown' (toasted cornmeal) and cocoyam pottage, gurgling in baby Fante talk, it was a long time before I returned to Ghana in 2014. But food was my guiding point, leading me to be reunited with those people who first informed my palate.

At the time of my return to Ghana, I had already started a well-received supper club and pop-up called Zoe's Ghana Kitchen and I was studying for my MA in Creative Writing at Goldsmiths, University of London, so the purpose of my trip was research, both for my portfolio and for my burgeoning food business. Prior to this, I had relied on the dishes that my dad had cooked while I was growing up, and my mum's interpretations in his absences, to sate my craving for African food, and then on the kindness of my 'aunties', the Ridley Road Market Ghanaian grocery store owners, who were incredulous (me being light skinned) that I was anything to do with Ghana and bemused by my inquisitiveness about the ingredients they sold and what they used them for. I became a frequent flyer with these ladies, as they transported me to their various home towns in the Volta region, or Kumasi in the Ashanti region, to describe what their local dishes and delicacies were.

While I was born to a Ghanaian father, I spent the majority of my childhood holidays in Ireland with my mother's family – all our summer and Easter vacations were spent building tree houses in rural West Cork, digging potatoes in my grandfather's small field, and collecting mussels from the beach at Bantry Bay, which was idyllic in some ways.

Back at home in South East London, my dad often brought home weird and wonderful exotic ingredients I had never been formally introduced to. Often he bought them to cook for himself, and he didn't seem to understand why I would be interested to know what they were, so I would have to quiz and bother him to gather as much information as I could.

My first (and only) cookery lesson was when Dad was cooking his chalé (spicy tomato) sauce. He had unceremoniously thrown into a pan his not-very-finely-chopped onions and his customary chilli and curry powder, and the smell and sizzle was fascinating. Next, his tomato mixture was sploshed in as I stood guard, and about 20 minutes later the splashback was splattered with hot tomato sauce. Concerned, I asked 'How do you know when it's done, Dad?' He casually walked over to the hob, looked at the splashback and explained, laughing: 'When it's up there, it's done!'

I remember standing next to him as he unwrapped kenkey (fermented corn dough) from its maize leaf casing and released that heady fermented odour, enquiring with an upturned nose, 'What is it, Dad?' I enviously watched him devouring the kenkey with tilapia and lashings of shito (hot pepper sauce) and wanted in. This is what started my food journey – connecting with my dad; connecting with my Ghanaian heritage.

I started cooking at home when I was relatively young and shared some of those dishes with friends. My school friend Lisa was the first fan of my peanut butter stew and other friends soon became eager for it. In fact, it was this particular dish, based on the traditional Ghanaian groundnut soup called nkatsenkwan ('stew' and 'soup' are interchangeable in Ghanaian cooking), that became the item that launched Zoe's Ghana Kitchen back in 2011 during the Hackney WickED Arts Festival. It remains my signature dish to this day in its various forms (*see* page 150 for the recipe).

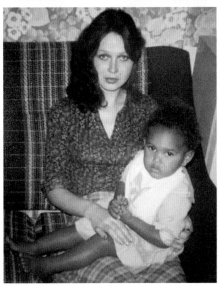

Regional Foods

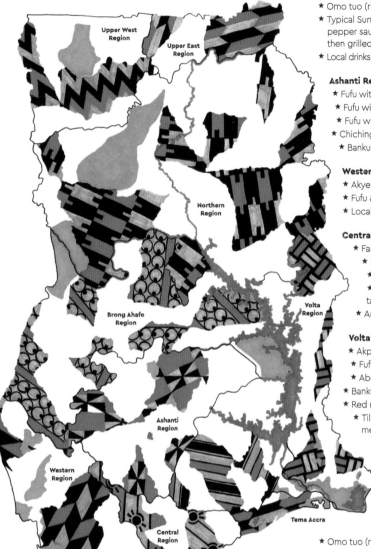

Greater Accra
- ★ Kenkey with hot pepper & fish
- ★ Banku with fried fish & pepper; okra or groundnut soup
- ★ Red red or yo-ko-gari (bean stew) with fried plantain or tatale
- ★ Omo tuo (rice balls) with palm or groundnut soup
- ★ Typical Sunday treat: fried yam with chofi (turkey tails) & hot, fresh pepper sauce; kebabs (meat or liver) doused in spicy powder then grilled
- ★ Local drinks: asana or maize beer; palm wine; coconut juice; akpeteshie

Ashanti Region (all about fufu)
- ★ Fufu with light soup
- ★ Fufu with smoked fish
- ★ Fufu with groundnut soup
- ★ Chichinga (spicy kebabs by the roadside)
- ★ Banku & grilled tilapia

Western Region
- ★ Akyene (cassava based) served with avocado
- ★ Fufu & light soup with mushrooms or snails
- ★ Local drinks: coconut juice; palm wine; akpeteshie

Central Region
- ★ Fante dorkunu (kenkey with fish & gravy)
- ★ Fufu & palmnut soup
- ★ Jollof rice
- ★ Fante fante (palm oil stew with small fresh fish) & a side of tatale (fried plantain cakes)
- ★ Ampesi (boiled plantains) or oto (mashed yam & eggs)

Volta Region
- ★ Akpla with okra soup
- ★ Fufu with palmnut soup
- ★ Abolo with shrimps & one man thousand
- ★ Banku with okra stew or pepper
- ★ Red red & fried plantain
- ★ Tilapia (a speciality which can be found roadside or on the menu of any shop or bar along the length of the Volta)

Brong Ahafo Region
- ★ Fufu with nkontomire (groundnut) soup, plantain & cocoyam ampesi

Northern Region
- ★ Tuo zafi (known as TZ) a spicy fish stock made with green leaves (usually taro)
- ★ Omo tuo (rice cakes) with groundnut or green leaves soup
- ★ Tubaani beans or cowpea with sheanut oil & pepper
- ★ Koko (millet/corn porridge) with koose (fried bean cakes)
- ★ Local drinks: pito (a locally-brewed beer made from millet, zom kroom & toasted millet flour with water); fula mashed with water, ginger & sugar

Upper East & West Regions
- ★ Tuo Zafi
- ★ Omo tuo with groundnut or green leaves soup
- ★ Tubaani
- ★ Koko with koose
- ★ Local drinks: pito; zom kroom

Eastern Region
- ★ A melting pot of all the above with a rich & diverse diet, from fufu to omo tuo and all the soups & stews inbetween.

Some Notes from My Kitchen

★ Sourcing ingredients responsibly

I am aware of the carbon footprint in using ingredients imported from Ghana, and I am therefore an advocate of choosing organic, free-range, locally sourced and sustainably produced ingredients wherever possible. So I encourage you to cook with a conscience and refer to my list of recommended stockists (see pages 254–5) when shopping for ingredients featured in the book.

★ Time-saving – when and when not to

The fact that traditional farming and harvesting methods are employed in the production of Ghanaian food means that much of it is relatively unprocessed. However, if, for example, a recipe calls for you to soak and then boil dried beans, it is entirely acceptable to use the canned variety to save time and effort (but do choose organically farmed products whenever you can).

I've devised shorthand versions of many of the traditional recipes, but some Ghanaian dishes are a labour of love and you just need to make the time – it's worth it! That said, I've also included a 'cheat sheet' that can help speed up cooking times (see pages 242–9), as we often simply don't have the time to slow-cook something for hours.

★ Seasonings of choice
Sea salt and freshly ground black pepper are my recommendations for basic seasoning. Try to use fresh herbs where possible. If you're substituting dried herbs, halve the quantity stated, as they are more potent in flavour.

★ Choosing and using ginger
I buy organic fresh root ginger and leave the skin on, as I find that it gives a stronger flavour. Try to buy the smaller African or Indian ginger rather than the huge, bloated stems that are common these days because, again, they have a more intense flavour profile.

★ Choosing and using yams and plantain
See pages 32 and 40 for my tips on buying and using yams and plantains to make sure you choose the appropriate quality and degree of ripeness for what you're cooking.

★ Cooking times
I cook with gas, so be aware that the cooking times specified may vary if using other cooking appliances.

★ Rice
Where long-grain white rice is used, cooking times relate to basmati rice for the purposes of consistency, but it's perfectly OK to use other long-grain white or brown rice instead; just adjust the cooking times according to the packet instructions.

★ Oils
I'm not a fan of fads in cooking, that said rapeseed oil has been a revelation for salad dressings and light frying. It can also be cheaper than equivalent quality olive oil, but wherever it appears feel free to use a good-quality olive oil instead.

There's an ongoing question mark over palm oil – in terms of its healthiness, its impact on the environment, and its sustainability. Following an aggressive government campaign in Ghana against palm oil – thought to be a factor in high cholesterol among the population – there has been a decline in it's use. But you can find evidence to support its antioxidant benefits also. I guess – as with all other oils – this is down to the quality and quantity of the oil you use. For me there are certain dishes that simply cannot exist without palm oil or a close equivalent such as carotene oil (Red Red Stew or Palm Soup for example). I know there are sustainable farming methods employed in Australia and New Zealand – please see the list of stockists and preferred suppliers for my recommendations on where to buy sustainable palm oil and equivalents.

Happy cooking!
Zoe x

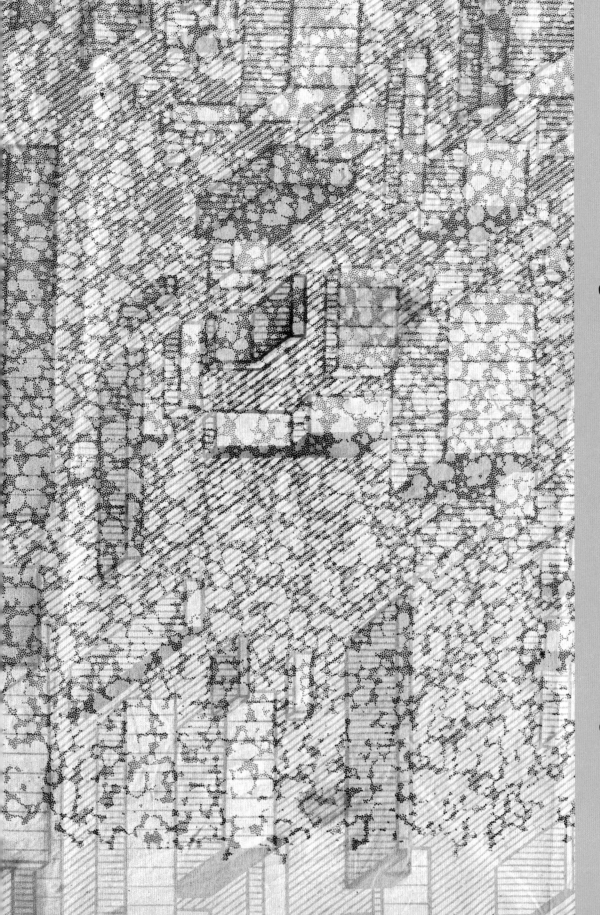

★ Guide to ingredients

Spices & Herbs

★ I'm often asked what is the 'holy trinity' – the three basic ingredients – of Ghanaian cooking. In Spanish and Italian or South American cooking it is *sofrito* – onion, garlic and tomatoes – while in French cooking it is mirepoix: onion, carrot and celery. The answer is surprisingly simple for Ghanaian cooking, too: onion, fresh root ginger and chilli added to tomatoes. Since I have never come across a name for this killer combo of ingredients that underpins so much of Ghanaian cuisine, I call my own recipe chalé sauce. Think of it as a sort of easy-to-make Ghanaian tomato sauce that can be used as the base for hundreds of different recipes (see page 247).

In Ghana, chalé means 'friend' or the equivalent of 'mate' to the British, but it's also used as an expression of disappointment, regret or resignation: 'Oh, chalé'. My dad's name is Kofi, but his English name is Charles, so when I was younger and I answered the phone to hear his Ghanaian friends saying 'Chalé', I thought they were saying Charlie. It wasn't until many years later that I realized they were saying 'Hey, chalé!'.

Besides the relatively simple 'holy trinity' that flavours chalé sauce, there is an abundance of wonderful spices and herbs native to West Africa that are incorporated into cooking and used repeatedly. The problem for me has been in pinpointing their names, given that there are so many different dialects among the 250 languages spoken in Ghana. To take one example, for a long time I couldn't get past the ubiquitous name 'shito' used to describe any sort of chilli or hot pepper, but some persistent enquiries among my family, and with Ghanaian market traders both in London and in Kaneshie, Accra, has allowed me to create a list of sorts (no doubt incomplete), which I now share with you.

You'll note that almost every indigenous spice has both a cooking and medicinal purpose and also that there are many spices and herbs used in Ghana that are common to cooking worldwide.

You may be surprised to learn that many of the fresh herbs listed here are available in Ghana, as most are not indigenous. Since their introduction by European, South American or Asian traders, they have become incorporated into Ghanaian daily life and it's not uncommon for most of them, along with vegetables, to be grown communally in compounds – something akin to allotments with homes dotted around them.

All of the ingredients listed on the following pages are available to buy in selected supermarkets and online (see Stockists, page 254–5).

CHILLIES (pictured below)

Shito, or shitor, is the catch-all name for any type of chilli in Ghana as well as for specific types of chilli or hot pepper sauces and dips – so not confusing at all!

Chillies, or hot peppers, appear widely in Ghanaian cooking, but not always to make dishes super-hot as some might think – they are often used to season meat and fish, stews and soups.

1 AFRICAN BIRD/DEVIL PEPPER (BIRD'S-EYE CHILLI) This easily recognizable member of the Capsicum family is more commonly known in the West as the bird's-eye chilli or sometimes Thai chilli. As with most small chillies, these fellas pack a fiery punch, and unlike the citrusy sweet fire of the habanero or Scotch Bonnet (see below and right), it's just pure heat, so use with caution! Medicinally, these chillies are reputed to help reduce blood pressure, ease stomach upsets and aid digestion.

2 HABANERO CHILLI This is the less-hot cousin of the Scotch Bonnet (see right).

3 KPAKPO SHITO (CHERRY) CHILLI A variety of *Capsicum chinense* Jacq, this chilli has its own distinctive taste. Don't be deceived by its cute size and inviting colour – while slightly milder than a bird's-eye pepper or Scotch Bonnet, it's a little ball of sweet fire. It makes a wonderful zingy salsa that bears the same name as the chilli itself (see page 231).

4 RED ROCKET (ANAHEIM) CHILLI This chilli originates from New Mexico. It adds a mild, fresh heat to your cooking if you prefer to go low on the Scoville scale and is great for a garnish, too.

5 SCOTCH BONNET CHILLI This is my FAVOURITE chilli and used in about 70 per cent of my recipes. But for those who don't like too much heat, don't worry, as it's optional most of the time. Scotch Bonnet chillies have a very specific smoky, sweet flavour and a heat that builds gradually when slowly cooked, without overpowering the dish. Eat it raw, though, and it will blow your head off!

(Spices & Herbs continued; pictured on pages 18–19)

1 BESE (KOLA NUTS)

Kola nuts are a common sight in Ghanaian markets in cities and villages, often sold by street hawkers. I once sat on a long bus trip up to Ho, the capital of Ghana's Volta region, next to a man who was ploughing through a bag of kola nuts and he offered me one. Taking his knife to break it open and cutting it into easily chewable segments for me, the bitter-tasting ball of caffeine – like a strong espresso capsule – kept me awake the whole journey when I all I wanted to do was sleep!

Kola nuts are best known outside Africa as an ingredient in cola beverages, made famous, of course, by Coca-Cola's commercial production of what was traditionally a simple West African recipe of water mixed with dried or fermented kola nuts (see page 217 for my Homemade Kola recipe). In their raw form they are somewhat difficult to find outside of Ghana, though some specialist/import grocery stores sell them (see Stockists, page 254–5). High in caffeine, kola nuts act as a stimulant and antidepressant, and are also reputed to reduce fatigue and hunger, aid digestion and work as an aphrodisiac.

CALABASH NUTMEG (AFRICAN NUTMEG)

Calabash is Africa's indigenous variety of nutmeg, so you might know it as African or Jamaican nutmeg, or *ehuru* (Nigeria). The fruits are collected from wild trees and then the seeds removed and dried. Inside, the fruit has a veined red helmet that resembles something from a comic hero's costume! The seeds are sold whole or ground to be used in stews, soups, cakes and desserts.

The smell and taste of calabash nutmeg is very similar to the common variety, though it perhaps has a deeper woodiness, and its flavour is intensified when toasted.

Calabash is said to have many medicinal properties ranging from relieving constipation to repelling insects.

2 CINNAMON

Introduced to West Africa by European traders, cinnamon is a widely used spice and features in the favourite Ghanaian spice rub known as *suya* (see page 246) as well as the Nigerian spice mix called *tsire* for grilled or barbecued meat.

3 CLOVES

These are the dried flower buds of the clove tree, *Syzygium aromaticum*, which originates from the Maluku Islands (historically known as the Spice Islands) in Indonesia, from where the Portuguese transported it to the East African islands. Today, it's a common spice in African cooking, and is also one of the ingredients in my Ghanaian Five-spice Mix (see page 244).

4 CUBEB PEPPER (JAVA PEPPER/TAILED PEPPER)

Africa's version of black pepper, cubeb pepper or tailed pepper (*Piper cubeba*), also referred to as Java pepper due to its Indonesian origin, has a woody pine tree aroma with a mild, peppery, clove-like flavour and a slightly bitter aftertaste. Once baked, cubeb pepper loses its bitterness and takes on a more rounded, complex flavour with hints of nutmeg and cardamom making it great for baking (*see* Cubeb Spiced Shortbread, page 179), although it's most frequently used to flavour vegetables and meat stews.

Used medicinally, it is reputed to act as an appetite stimulant and relieve constipation and indigestion.

5 CUMIN

Cumin seeds are the dried seeds of a herb (*Cuminum cyminum*) that was first cultivated in Ancient Egypt. It was originally used in the cuisines of the northern region of the African continent but was later introduced to Central Africa. It is commonly used to flavour sauces to accompany chicken and other meat dishes.

6 CURRY POWDER

Curry powder is a mix of several spices widely used in Ghanaian vegetable, meat and fish dishes.

7 FENNEL SEEDS

When I last visited Ghana, I was surprised to see fennel seeds among the local market produce. A particular genus that is able to withstand extreme heat is imported from India, grown and harvested in Ghana – who knew?

Used in some fish stews, consumption of fennel seeds increases in the summer months of March to June, as they are cooling and refreshing in taste. This inoffensive seed is also a remedy for flatulence and indigestion in traditional medicinal practice. Amusingly, it is also sometimes called the 'meeting seed', as it is customarily chewed by congregations during long church services to keep them awake!

8 GARLIC

Again, surprisingly common and grown in small compounds, it's origins lie in Asia but the early Egyptians were flagbearers of its use before it spread to the Mediterranean.

9 GINGER

This is another seasoning originating from Asia, in this case Southeast Asia, and was imported from India via Egypt by the Ancient Romans to become their favourite spice. The fact that ginger was a root, and therefore could be relatively easily shipped, meant that its use quickly spread to other parts of the world including the Caribbean and Africa, where it's a commonly used ingredient in cooking. Non-alcoholic beer and other drinks are also made from ginger throughout the continent, but particularly in the west.

GROUND HOT PEPPER

This is referred to in a lot of my recipes. It's an African chilli blend that is most like cayenne pepper, so substitute it with this if you can't source any.

10 HWENTEA (GUINEA PEPPER/ETHIOPIAN PEPPER/GRAINS OF SELIM/SENEGAL PEPPER)

This spice comes from the fruits of a shrubby tree, *Xylopia aethiopica*, found in Africa. Its woody pods contain little black seeds that have a musky, aromatic flavour that reminds me of stepping into an aromatherapy session. Guinea pepper is commonly used in the making of Shito (Hot Pepper Sauce – *see* page 228) but can also be infused into warming drinks (*see* Guinea Pepper & Ginger Tea, page 221).

The pods can be crushed or cracked open – with a little difficulty! – and added whole to soups and stews (*see*, for example, Nkrakra/Light Soup with Chicken, page 129, and Lamb Palaver, page 136), then removed before serving, while the smoked pods can be ground before being used as a spice rub for fish.

11 MESEWA (GRAINS OF PARADISE/ALLIGATOR PEPPER/MELEGUETA PEPPER)

Native to West Africa, this spice has the botanical name *Aframomum melegueta* and is a member of the ginger family *Zingiberaceae*. Its tiny, round grains reminiscent of miniature nutmegs are seeds, easily harvested from leafy plants. Commonly known as grains of paradise because it was claimed by medieval spice traders that these peppery seeds grew only in Eden, and had to be collected as they floated down the river out of Paradise.

Once crushed, the seeds release a pungent citrusy aroma with hints of jasmine and cardamom. If you bite into one, you'll notice that the peppery heat slowly intensifies and develops on the palate. They are great used as a spice rub for fish, especially if you toast them in a dry frying pan before crushing (*see* Pan-roasted Cod Seasoned with Grains of Paradise, page 68). Grains of paradise are also said to have aphrodisiac qualities.

12 RED SORREL (DRIED HIBISCUS FLOWERS)

Red sorrel (*Hibiscus sabdariffa*) is a red flowering plant that grows abundantly in Ghana and bizarrely enough is a cousin of okra. The dried, prickly, intense red flowers make a wonderfully vibrant show, overflowing from huge woven baskets or sacks in the market places. Its most popular culinary use in Ghana is as an iced spicy ginger-flavoured drink called Sobolo (*see* page 214).

It is traditionally used across Africa in the treatment of a number of health problems, such as to reduce blood pressure, stimulate liver function and as a diuretic. The red sorrel flower is high in essential vitamins and minerals, including vitamin C, calcium and niacin (a B vitamin used to increase HDL, the 'good' cholesterol), and modern research has shown that red sorrel contains powerful antioxidants that help rid the body of disease-causing free radicals. It has also been found to reduce the risk of heart disease, helping to prevent the clogging of arteries by significantly reducing elevated cholesterol levels.

Pulses, Grains & Legumes

★ Some of the major staples of Ghanaian cooking include beans, lentils, rice and other kinds of grain.

BEANS

Beans are used in several types of dishes, such as soups, stews, rice dishes and salads, and as snacks. Those most commonly used are black-eyed, mung and red kidney beans.

ABORBOI (BAMBARA BEANS) bambara beans (*Vigna subterranea*), or bambara groundnuts, are grown widely across West Africa and known by many different names in each country, called *aborboi* by many in Ghana. The plant is ploughed out or hoed from the ground and the nuts then pulled off. Though they can be eaten raw, they are usually dried and boiled much like a pulse. Being a hardy plant able to thrive in tough, arid conditions also means that the beans take a long time to cook and usually require overnight soaking beforehand. The bean's most famous use is in Aboboi (see page 107) – a bambara bean stew served with Tatale (plantain pancakes, see page 43). The beans are also roasted and milled to make flour, and as they are high in protein, are used as an affordable livestock feed.

BLACK-EYED BEANS also called cowpeas, are indigenous to the continent of Africa, where they are a staple food. Beans are generally grown on a small scale in compound gardens.

DRIED LENTILS AND PEAS

Nowadays lentils are imported from India and Asia into Africa and are used all over the continent, as in the rest of the world. They are usually soaked overnight, boiled and mashed together with other vegetables to be used as an accompaniment to a meat or fish dish.

YELLOW DRIED SPLIT PEAS These were surprisingly common in the kitchens I visited in Accra and Ho, added to stews and soups – check out my recipe for Ghana Dhal (see page 108).

MILLET

While millets, a widely varied group of grasses with small seeds, are indigenous to many parts of the world, it is believed that they originally evolved in tropical Western Africa, as that is where the greatest number of both wild and cultivated forms exist. They are highly tolerant of extreme weather conditions such as drought, and are nutritious compared with the other major cereals like wheat and rice.

Cooked millet appears in the breakfast favourite of *hausa koko* – a millet porridge – and is also eaten widely in the northern regions as part of *tuo zaafi*, meaning 'very hot' (this dish is often shortened to 'TZ'). Millet meal is used in the same way as rice balls, banku and kenkey as the carbohydrate component to a dish.

Also see Sorghum Leaves/Dried Millet on page 29.

RICE

Rice is an important staple in the Ghanaian diet. It is mainly grown in swampy lowlands under standing water on community or privately-owned fields, but also on a large scale on irrigated government, community or privately-owned plantations. However, much of the rice consumed in Africa comes from cheap imports or donations from Asia, which has resulted in basmati becoming the preferred grain.

Other Staple Ingredients & Flavourings (pictured on pages 22-23)

★ The below make up the basis of many meal accompaniments and flavour enhancers most commonly used in Ghanaian cuisine.

1 AGUSHI/AKATOA (DRIED MELON SEEDS)

Full of protein and vitamins, these can be ground and added to soups or stews to create a creamy texture (see Kontomire & Apem Stew, page 95, Spinach & Agushi, page 102, and Lamb Palaver, page 136).

2 AMANE (SMOKED/DRIED FISH)

Smoked, dried fish or crustaceans, such as mackerel, prawns and crayfish are a very common food enhancer, most often ground into a powder to use as a seasoning in many dishes including Fetri Detsi (see page 135).

Dried and ground smoked herrings and prawns or crayfish can also be used to flavour Shito (see page 228), a very popular spicy Ghanaian condiment.

3 BANKU

This is fermented cornmeal that is cooked into a porridge-like dough ball and eaten as a side (see page 169) with soups and stews all across Africa, though it may go by different names. In the Caribbean it's known as 'turned cornmeal'.

4 DAWADAWA (AFRICAN LOCUST BEAN)

This is one powerfully odorous fermented ingredient and not for the faint-hearted, but African locust bean (Parkia biglobosa), also known as dawadawa, transforms into an effective flavour enhancer in many soups including Palm Soup (see page 110). It's mostly used in the northern regions of Ghana and is reputed to have innumerable health benefits, if you can bear the smell, including aiding the management of diabetes and hypertension, as well as being an antidote to snake bites – something to bear in mind!

5 DOKON (FANTE KENKEY)

This fermented corn dough is boiled and then wrapped in corn cob leaves (Ga kenkey), or plantain or banana leaves (Fante kenkey) and steamed for hours. A bit like banku (see left), it is served as a side to stews, more commonly fish-based dishes. A similar dish in the Caribbean is called duckanoo.

6 FUFU

Everybody loves fufu – the Ashanti people say a man has not eaten if he hasn't eaten fufu that day. It's the name given to vegetables such as steamed, pounded green plantain, cassava or a combination of both, but you can also make it with pounded yam, which is common in Nigeria. The high starch content of these root vegetables and green plantain gives the viscosity needed for the fufu dough to form, which means that it works less well if you try using yellow (ripe) plantain for this purpose.

'Instant' fufu or fufu flour (as pictured on page 23) is readily available – just follow the instructions on the packet to prepare, or use my recipe on page 173.

7 GROUNDNUTS

Groundnuts are quite simply the ubiquitous and delicious peanut, used in all forms of cooking including in stews, soups, spice rubs, snacks and desserts, and of course to make peanut butter and groundnut oil.

8 KOOBI (DRIED SALTED TILAPIA)

This is another ingredient not for everyone, because of its very strong odour. Used in soups, it's preferred over dawadawa (African locust bean) in southern Ghana. Just to be clear, this is not a matter of ethnic rivalry, it's just that southerners are situated along the coast where fish is readily available, whereas northerners have the African locust bean growing around them.

FRUITS (pictured on pages 26-27)

★ Africa is not an arid continent and has an extraordinary array of ecosystems including mangrove swamps, savannahs and rainforests. Each offer up an abundance of medicinal plants and even the savannahs and deserts contain fruit-bearing trees that are packed with nutrients and therapeutic value. The West has finally caught on to the power of Africa's traditional medicines and remedies that still effectively treat the great majority of the population. For example, you can now see moringa and baobab on the shelves of most supermarkets and health-food stores. Ghana's got fruit – and it's damn good fruit!

ADASAMA (AFRICAN STAR APPLE/WHITE STAR APPLE)

This fruit is associated with Christmas and New Year celebrations because it falls when ripe (rather than being picked) from December to March. Eaten as a snack, rather than being cooked, its tough, leather-like, skin is green to dark-orange and contains a reddish or orange flesh (depending on ripeness). It has a tart sour flesh that can be chewed with the sweet, white, latex-like sap as a sort of chewing gum to counterbalance the sourness.

A highly rich source of calcium, it also contains high doses of vitamins A and C and is rich in iron. The flesh of the fruit is said to possess chemical nutrients with similar properties to insulin, and so is believed to be effective in reducing blood sugar and cholesterol as well as helping to prevent and treat hypertension and heart disease.

1 BANANA

In its wild form this fruit is hard and full of seeds, but with domestication and cultivation it has become sweet and seedless. The Arabs began to grow the plant in parts of northern Africa in the Middle Ages, and the banana thus spread to the Iberian Peninsula. The Portuguese also 'discovered' the banana growing in Africa in the 15th century.

Bananas are commonly eaten without any special preparation and are mostly served at the end of a meal and often with peanuts.

Unripe (green) bananas are sometimes used as a green vegetable, mostly boiled with or without their skin.

BAOBAB (MONKEY BREAD)

Baobab is a 100 per cent natural and organic raw fruit from the baobab tree – or monkey bread tree, as it's known in Africa. It's the only fruit in the world that dries on the branch, producing a natural fruit powder that is packed with nutritional goodness, being both low in sugar and fat, yet high in fibre. It contains more than 12 minerals and vitamins, and just 1 tablespoon provides 33 per cent of your Recommended Daily Allowance (RDA) of vitamin C.

I cannot extoll the virtues of baobab enough, and it has a wonderful citrusy zest that will brighten up almost anything you add it to.

2 COCONUT

The coconut is truly a tropical fruit, from a large palm tree that spread of its own accord to tropical coastal zones all over the world. The flesh and milk from the coconut is widely used in African cooking, in relishes, fried dishes, sauces, desserts – you name it. Creamed coconut is grated on to casseroles or dissolved in water to make coconut milk. Fresh coconut is sometimes peeled into slivers and used as a topping for desserts.

3 GREEN PAPAYA/PAWPAW

Unripe papaya or pawpaw makes a great meat tenderizer – chop it up and add it to the pot in which you are cooking a tough cut of meat and it will soften it up. You can also marinate the meat in unripe papaya pulp before cooking. Papaya contains an enzyme called *papain*, which is commonly used in commercial meat-tenderizing products that you find on supermarket shelves.

4 PINEAPPLE

Of the three main types of pineapple grown in Ghana you won't find a sweeter, juicier pineapple than the Sugarloaf variety – ubiquitous in Ghanaian local markets. Rather sadly, the requirement for aesthetically-pleasing pineapples (largely dictated by supermarket and retail store chains) means that the exports of this variety from Ghana to Europe and North America are virtually nil. It's sister, the Smooth Cayenne, which is also sweet and juicy and a brighter yellow in colour, has all the markers of your common variety pineapple but is actually less good for juicing. If you get to Ghana - get your hands on some Sugarloaf!

5 MANGO

In Ghana, mangoes are harvested over a very short period – June to August – and have historically been quite unstable crops due to issues of transportation and storage. However, as demand for Ghanaian mangoes grows, efficient cultivation methods improve. There are many varieties of mango cultivated in Ghana, including the very smooth and firm Keitt, the very firm Haden, the more familiar Kent, which is juicy and tender, the fairly fibrous textured Tommy Atkins and the buttery Atualfo.

6 SOURSOP/CUSTARD APPLE

Soursop is a long, prickly, green fruit with a fleshy sweet white pulp surrounding a core of indigestible black seeds. Soursop is one of those super fruits – derivatives of which are consumed widely across the world but may not be very well known. The pulp is used to make fruit nectar, smoothies and fruit juice drinks, as well as sorbets and ice cream flavourings.

Soursop leaf and bark are consumed for their alternative health benefits, which are numerous and include immune-boosting properties inherent in its compounds, being rich in fibre and having a high calcium content to promote bone growth and health.

It is also said to cure haemorrhoids, while applying its flesh to fresh cuts is thought to aid healing and prevent bacterial infection.

Add a small quantity of soursop or 'graviola' leaves to Moringa Tea (*see* page 212) for a killer health food combo.

YOOY! (GHANA BLACKBERRIES/AFRICAN VELVET TAMARIND)

With the botanical name *Dialium guineense*, African velvet tamarind has in fact nothing to do with blackberries apart from a vaguely similar shape and perhaps the inherent sweetness and sharpness of its brown sticky pulp, which you reach by gently cracking open the pod.

In the upper west region of Ghana, the Waala people call tamarind *puhee* from which they make a refreshing drink (not unlike Sobolo, *see* page 214) named *puhikuong* meaning 'tamarind water'.

Boasting a wealth of health benefits but not necessarily really eaten for that purpose, it contains the powerful antioxidant tartaric acid, which apparently helps to remove body waste, while its high fibre content prevents constipation. Supposedly the leaf extract inhibits the growth of *Plasmodium falciparum* which causes malaria – what a wonder!

VEGETABLES (pictured on pages 30-31)

★ People are often surprised when I reel off the long list of vegetables that are available and widely used in Ghanaian cooking – they assume it's all meat. The Ghanaian climate is tropical but relatively mild, with two rainy seasons, and each region has it's own micro-climate for production of local vegetable crops. This list is restricted to those that are most-readily available outside Ghana and are used in the recipes in this book.

1 CASSAVA (MANIOC/TAPIOCA/BANKYE)

The cassava or manioc plant originated from South America, from where it was introduced to Africa by Portuguese explorers in the 16th century through their trade with the African coast and nearby islands. It is now found in almost all parts of tropical Africa.

If the yam resembles a log, then cassava looks like a stick or branch. Its waxy, brown, bark-like skin is a curiosity in itself and can be tricky to peel, which speaks of the hardiness that makes it resistant to locust attacks and drought. Inside its mysterious skin is a hard and starchy white flesh that, through a process of cooking, fermentation and drying, forms the basis of many staple foods in Ghanaian cooking – cassava flour is used to make Banku and Fufu (see pages 169 and 173) and, when fermented and ground, gari.

Interestingly, cassava contains cyanide, which needs to be eliminated during the preparation of the flour. Cooking or fermenting the vegetable removes the cyanide. See page 195 for my Coconut & Cassava Cake. You can find my Tip for preparing cassava on page 164.

2 COCOYAM

The cocoyam is part of the yam family but is much smaller and has a slightly hairy skin. It looks a little like a misshapen coconut, which is probably where it's name comes from. It's also slightly sweeter than puna yam (see page 32) and less starchy, which makes it easier to peel like a potato, boil and chop, but it's miniature size means that it's less easy to make into chips. See page 190 for my Cocoyam & Sweet Potato Curry.

3 GARDEN EGG (AFRICAN AUBERGINE/EGGPLANT)

Today, it's the large purple aubergine that features in the daily fare of Greeks and Egyptians, whereas it's the smaller, pale-coloured, egg-shaped African aubergine that is widely used in West Africa, which explains why it's called 'eggplant' or 'garden egg', although they also come in a variety of colours including yellow, pink, red, lavender and even striped. In Ghana the garden egg is known as *nyadua* in the Twi language, *ntrowa* or *ntoroba* in Fante and *agbitsa* in Ewe. They are chopped, cooked and mixed into a variety of vegetable, meat and fish dishes as well as sauces.

4 KONTOMIRE/NKONTOMIRE
(taro leaves)

Pronounced 'con-tom-ray', kontomire are the bitter leaves of the cocoyam plant, also known as taro leaves – nothing gets wasted in Ghana! They are used in dishes such as agushi (dried ground melon seed) stew (see Spinach & Agushi on page 102).

5 OKRA

Okra is an extremely popular vegetable in African cooking, often added to soups. It needs no special preparation besides washing, trimming and cutting up. It can be the nemesis to most palates because of it's traditional association as a slimy vegetable. See my recipes for Nkrumen (Pan-fried Okra), Nkruma (Okra) Tempura and Nkruma Nkwan (Okra Soup and Banku) on pages 204 and 182 for ways to cook okra to eliminate the slime!

6 ONION

Onions are an important element of almost every cooked dish in Ghanaian cooking, and one of the 'holy trinity' of key ingredients that form the basis of Chalé Sauce (see page 247).

PLANTAIN (see page 40)

7 SORGHUM LEAVES/DRIED MILLET
('WAAKYE')

These are used to impart a reddish colouring to the Ghanaian rice and beans dish known as Waakye Rice (see page 162). If you don't use these particular leaves, you're cooking regular rice and beans, not true waakye.

8 SWEET POTATO

While the sweet potato has its origins in tropical America, you can find them growing all across West Africa, having been introduced by European traders. As versatile as any good-quality regular potato, sweet potatoes can be boiled, roasted, fried, creamed or baked in their skins, and work equally well in sweet and savoury dishes. See Roasted & Stuffed Spiced Sweet Potato, page 104.

YAM (see page 32)

YAM 5 WAYS

★ Some people confuse the yam with the sweet potato. They are not the same. Yams resemble small logs – a tuber about the length of an adult forearm but often wider – and have either white or yellowish turnip-coloured flesh inside. There are over 200 species of yam (*Dioscorea*), but only a handful are suitable for cooking, including *Dioscorea esculenta*, of which Ghana's preferred variety is puna yam, a yellow-fleshed sweet yam, the other variety being white yam.

Some wild yam species are farmed by pharmaceutical companies for their purported anti-ageing properties and as a source of natural progesterone, and yam pills are marketed as a contraceptive and also to promote fertility.

Yam is an incredibly versatile root vegetable that can be prepared in as many ways as the potato (boiled, roasted, baked, mashed, made into chips and even puréed). As a child, yam was a common component of my dad's cooking, in the same way as potato was for my Irish mum. In fact, corned beef stew and yam is one of my all-time favourite dishes that Dad whipped up in just half an hour – a hearty, spiced concoction made with his chalé sauce and a can of corned beef, with boiled eggs plonked into the spluttering sauce and served with great slabs of overboiled yam on the side (see page 149). However much I loved this dish, I always wondered why the floury yam tasted so delicious yet looked so unappealing!

In this section we're going to look at just a few ways in which you can cook yams and incorporate them into some popular dishes.

Buying Yams

Although you can buy your yams from supermarkets these days, the quantities they sell are rather large, so if you buy from your local market you'll be better able to check the quality of the vegetable and purchase the exact quantity you need, avoiding waste and saving you unnecessary expense.

Yellow yam and white yam are deceptively similar from the outside.

When buying yams the expert way, you must first acknowledge the grocer with a nod or smile and then begin a slow, studied perusal. You need to be looking out for puna yam, the yam of the gods and Ghana's preferred yam, although you can substitute other varieties, but not sweet potato or cocoyam, which are different again (see page 28).

Next, you must handle more than one yam before making your choice – a close-up examination with both your eyes and hands. Look out for any signs of moulding – a bluish-green edge to parts of the skin, or black dots on the flesh of the yam if it's cut open at one end. Feel down the length of the yam for any sponginess or bruising, as you want a firm yam – try to make sure the grocer can see you doing this so that she or he knows you are a yam expert!

Ask your grocer to cut the ends off the yam to check that there is no rot hiding inside – yam has a very long shelf life, but if it isn't stored properly it can start to rot inside. To be sure this hasn't happened, ask the grocer to cut the yam in half to check the centre – it should be a nice white moist disc. A good grocer will be confident of the freshness of their product so shouldn't deny you, and if you have followed all the steps above, they'll think you're a pro!

★ Fried yam is a massively popular snack and side dish in Ghana, and it's super easy to make variations on the theme. Try this French toast-style recipe that my fiancée suggested I should devise.

Savoury Fried Yam

450g (1lb) puna yam

cooking salt

4–6 eggs

½ teaspoon sea salt

½ teaspoon freshly ground black pepper

¼ teaspoon ground hot pepper, or substitute cayenne pepper, or to taste

1 tablespoon rapeseed oil or sunflower oil

Have a bowl or pan of water ready before you start, as you'll need to put each peeled yam piece straight into water as you go to prevent them oxidizing and turning brown. Peel the yam and cut 4 discs about 1cm (½ inch) thick, then rinse thoroughly in cold water to remove the starch.

Cut each disc in half and add them to a saucepan of lightly salted boiling water to cover. Cook for 10–15 minutes or until just fork tender. Drain and leave the yam to cool.

Break the eggs into a bowl, add the sea salt, black pepper and chilli powder or cayenne pepper and beat well with a fork.

Heat the oil in a nonstick frying pan over a medium-high heat. Dip the yam slices, individually or a few at a time if the bowl is large enough, in the beaten egg mixture.

When the oil in the pan is hot, add the yam slices to the pan and allow them to brown on the underside. When you notice the edges starting to brown, turn over and cook until browned on the other side. Serve warm.

→ **TIPS** For variation, use a little palm oil or carotene oil to fry.

You can also add onion, thinly sliced, to the egg mixture for coating the yam slices before frying. Or for simple good old-fashioned fried yam, simply omit the eggs and fry the boiled yam slices in the frying pan with the onion.

★ These crunchy balls of goodness make for a great starter, especially served with an assortment of dips or salsas, such as Shito (Hot Pepper Sauce) and Green Kpakpo Shito Salsa (see pages 228 and 231), or a green salad. They are very simple to make and you can change up what you season them with every time (see Tips, below) or use diced pepper instead of onion.

Bankye Akakro
Mashed Yam Balls with a Gari Crust

450g (1lb) puna yam

cooking salt

75g (2¾oz) butter or spread, for mashing

1 tablespoon smoked paprika

1 small red onion, finely chopped

3 spring onions, finely chopped

1 garlic clove, very finely chopped

1 tablespoon thyme leaves

sea salt and freshly ground black pepper

4 egg yolks, beaten

50-75g (1¾-2¾oz) cornflour seasoned with salt and pepper for coating, plus **1 tablespoon** (unseasoned) if required

100g (3½oz) gari (fermented, dried and ground cassava)

500ml-1 litre (18fl oz-1¾ pints) vegetable oil, for deep-frying

Have a bowl or pan of water ready before you start, as you'll need to put each peeled yam piece straight into water as you go to prevent them oxidizing and turning brown. Slice the yam into discs 2cm (¾ inch) thick and then peel as if peeling an apple. Chop each disc into 2.5cm (1-inch) cubes, then rinse thoroughly in cold water to remove the starch.

Add the yam chunks to a saucepan of salted boiling water and cook for 12–15 minutes until just fork tender.

Drain well, rinse again and mash the yam with the butter or spread and smoked paprika, then leave to cool.

While the yam is cooling, you can prepare a salsa or side salad to go with the balls (see the recipe introduction).

Tip the yam mash into a large bowl, add the red onion and spring onions, garlic, thyme, sea salt and black pepper to taste. Add about half the beaten egg yolks and beat together. You want a very smooth mash, so you may want to add the 1 tablespoon cornflour to achieve the right consistency.

Put the seasoned cornflour in a shallow bowl or deep plate, the remaining beaten egg yolks in a second bowl and the gari in a third bowl. Form the mixture into plum-sized balls. First roll each ball in the seasoned flour, then submerge in the egg yolks and finally roll immediately in the gari, ensuring that it is fully coated to create a crunchy outside – repeat the coating process if necessary.

Chill the yam balls in the fridge for at least an hour to firm up and allow the egg mixture to dry.

Heat the oil for deep-frying in a deep-fat fryer (the safest option) or heavy-based, deep saucepan filled to just under half the depth of the pan to 170–180°C (340–350°F). Deep-fry the yam balls, in batches, for 2 minutes until golden, turning once. Remove from the oil and drain on kitchen paper, keeping the cooked balls hot while you fry the rest.

→ **TIPS** *You can also turn the yam mixture into yam cakes by moulding it into patties rather than balls.*

I use smoked paprika for the gentle heat it provides, but you can add chopped fresh chillies instead or swap for a fragrant spice such as ground turmeric or cumin.

★ Oto (pronounced 'oh-tow') is a classic Ghanaian celebratory dish always made with hard-boiled eggs, mashed yam and palm oil, and served in particular on occasions such as naming ceremonies for newborn babies, birthdays, or wedding breakfasts.

SERVES 4-6

I found out about this dish on a trip to Ghana when I saw my Aunt Evelyn's wedding photos. Evelyn told me that 'her people' – that is Ga people (most of my family are Fante) – eat oto for breakfast on their wedding day to give them the energy to keep them upstanding throughout the long day of the ceremony. Which makes perfect sense, since yam has a very high starch content and will therefore help to keep you fuelled all day long if you eat a big enough portion.

Oto
Golden Mashed Yam

750–900g (1lb 10oz–2lb) puna yam

cooking salt

4–6 hard-boiled eggs, shelled and quartered

120ml (4fl oz) sustainable palm oil or carotene oil

2 red onions, 1 finely diced and 1 sliced and fried in palm oil or carotene oil to serve as a garnish or side

1–2 tablespoons dried ground prawn/shrimp powder (optional)

a little butter, if required

sea salt, to taste if required

chopped spring onion or coriander, to garnish

Baked or Crispy Fried Kale (see page 200), to serve (optional)

Have a bowl or pan of water ready, as you'll need to put each peeled yam piece straight into water to prevent them oxidizing and turning brown. Peel the yam and cut into 2.5–5cm (1–2-inch) cubes, then rinse thoroughly in cold water to remove the starch.

Add the yam cubes to a large saucepan of lightly salted boiling water and cook for 12–15 minutes, depending on the thickness of the yam, until fork tender. (You can hard-boil your eggs in the pan at the same time to save on the washing-up!) Drain and mash the yam (set the hard-boiled eggs aside for garnish).

Heat the palm oil in a heavy-based saucepan, add the diced onion and sauté over a medium heat for a few minutes until soft. Add the prawn/shrimp powder (if using) and stir to combine.

Remove the pan from the heat and gradually add the oil and onions to the mashed yam, stirring and mixing thoroughly. If you're finding it tough going – yam is a heavy-duty vegetable to mash – add a little butter.

Continue adding the oil and onions until the yam mixture is an even bright saffron colour and a dense mash texture, but not a purée. You may not need to use all the oil, so taste and add extra oil and sea salt if required.

Serve in individual bowls with the hard-boiled egg and the fried sliced red onion on top, with a green garnish such as chopped spring onion or coriander, or to really bring out the richness of the colour, serve alongside a portion of baked or Crispy Fried Kale.

If you want to eat oto the authentic way, use your hands to make small balls of the mash and chow down from a communal bowl. Swift lesson in Ghanaian eating etiquette, as taught to me by my Aunt Evelyn: always use your right hand when eating – especially in communal dining – as the right is considered 'clean', while the left is considered 'dirty'. Aunt Evelyn is Ga, so I'm not sure if that's a Ga thing, but don't risk it! Also, provide individual finger bowls of warm water and lemon to rinse the fingers between mouthfuls.

★ If you've ever eaten Peruvian food, you will probably have tried cassava fries or chips. Yam, like cassava, is a type of starchy, tubular root vegetable akin to the staple potato in the Ghanaian diet. There are many varieties, but few that are edible. Puna yam is the Ghanaian version of the superior King Edward potato – it's very fluffy and slightly sweet when cooked properly and can be chipped, boiled, mashed and so on, in the same way. Serve these chips with Lamb Cutlets with Peanut Sauce, some Shito (Hot Pepper Sauce) and Green Kpakpo Shito Salsa (see pages 122, 228 and 231) or a green salad.

Chunky Yam Chips

650g (1lb 7oz) puna yam

cooking salt

2 tablespoons sunflower oil

1 teaspoon sea salt, or to taste

smoked paprika or cayenne pepper, (optional)

Have a bowl or pan of water ready before you start, as you'll need to put each peeled yam piece straight into water as you go to prevent them oxidizing and turning brown. Slice the yam into discs 2cm (¾ inch) thick and then peel as if peeling an apple. Chop each disc into chips 1–2cm (½–¾ inch) thick – about 4–5 chips per disc if you've bought a thick yam. Rinse thoroughly in cold water to remove the starch.

Add the yam chips to a large saucepan of lightly salted boiling water and blanch for 8–10 minutes until fork soft. This is in order just to break down the starch structure and the chips need to stay firm – overboiling them by even a minute will cause them to fall apart, so keep a close eye on them. If you're worried about overcooking them, you can alternatively soak the chips in water for about 20 minutes. This blanching method speeds things up and also ensures that the centre of the chips will be nice and fluffy once baked or fried.

Drain the chips well and gently shake them as you do so, allowing the outsides to slightly fluff up, which will crisp up wonderfully when you bake or fry them. Leave the steam to rise off the chips while they cool. Don't rinse them again!

While the yam is cooling, you can prepare a salsa or side salad to go with the chips (see the recipe introduction). Also, preheat the oven to 180°C (350°F), Gas Mark 4.

Line a large baking tray with greaseproof paper and spread out the cooled yam chips so that there is a little space between each. Sprinkle the yams with the oil and sea salt to your taste – I also like to sprinkle them with some smoked paprika or cayenne pepper to give them a punch – making sure they are evenly coated with the oil and seasoning.

Bake the chips for 30–40 minutes, turning them over halfway through the cooking time. You should now have some delicious baked yam chips!

→ **TIP** For a triple-cooked chip, which is my preference, heat 500ml–1 litre (18fl oz–1¾ pints) sunflower oil for deep-frying in a deep-fat fryer (the safest option) or heavy-based, deep saucepan filled to just under half the depth of the pan to 180–190°C (350–375°F) or until a cube of bread browns in 30 seconds. Deep-fry the baked yam chips, in batches, for 2 minutes until golden. Remove from the oil and drain on kitchen paper, keeping the cooked chips hot while you fry the rest.

★ The floury texture of boiled yam makes it akin to the famous Irish potato and it can be a great addition to curries and potages. This recipe combines my love of Nkatsenkwan (groundnut stew – see page 150) with the two simple Ghanaian staples of yam and plantain. This was the way I ate it as a child, when the lamb had gone from the pot and there was always leftover peanut sauce (both my mum and dad cooked it in great vats), which you could then add to some boiled yam and plantain. It makes a great alternative veggie curry!

Yam & Plantain Peanut Curry

300g (10½oz) puna yam

cooking salt

2-3 medium-ripe plantains, peeled and cut into large chunks

1 quantity Peanut Sauce, prepared up to the stage of adding the peanut butter and blending (see page 249)

TO GARNISH

chopped red chillies

sliced spring onions or puréed basil

Have a bowl or pan of water ready before you start, as you'll need to put each peeled yam piece straight into water as you go to prevent them oxidizing and turning brown. Peel the yam and cut into slices, then rinse thoroughly in cold water to remove the starch.

Chop the yam, add to a large saucepan of lightly salted boiling water and cook for 10 minutes.

Meanwhile, peel the plantains and cut into chunks slightly larger than bite size. Add to the boiling yam at the 10-minute point and cook together for about a further 10 minutes until fork tender – they will continue to cook in the peanut sauce.

Strain, reserving the cooking water to use as vegetable stock for making the peanut sauce. Set the yam and plantain aside.

Follow the method on page 249 to prepare the peanut sauce, using the reserved cooking water for the stock, up to and including the stage of adding the peanut butter and blending until smooth. Add the boiled yam and plantain to the sauce and leave to simmer for 20 minutes, stirring in a little water as necessary to prevent any sticking.

Serve in a bowl garnished with chopped red chillies and a touch of greenery such as sliced spring onions or puréed basil.

Yam & Plantain
Peanut Curry

Oto

Savoury Fried Yam

Bankye Akakro

Chunky Yam Chips

PLANTAIN 5 WAYS

★ The plantain is a member of the banana family, and the fruits can be green, yellow or almost black depending on their degree of ripeness. When plantains are green and unripe, they have a chalky texture and taste resembling the potato. Plantains should not be eaten raw, but once boiled, fried, baked or roasted, they have a wonderful flavour. They are mostly grown on a small scale in compound gardens.

I think there are probably a hundred recipes alone for cooking plantain. It has such a long life span in which its textures and flavours mature that, at each stage of its life, there is some method of cooking to employ to get the best from its life cycle.

What colour plantain?

Over a six- to eight-week period - from the time it falls starch-heavy and green from the branch to the completely overripe, all-black, naturally sweet and caramelized state – there is a best way to cook and eat plantain. You could say it's the fruit that keeps on giving, but it's important to use the right type of plantain for the recipe.

Green plantain is the least delicious stage for me, though it can be wondrously transformed from a rigid starchy and difficult-to-peel stubborn vegetable through boiling to make Apem, or pounding to make plantain fufu – it's most commonly used when fallen fresh from the tree.

At this point in the cycle it is typically extremely low in fat and high in dietary fibre and starch, as well as being low in cholesterol and salt. It's the high starch content in green plantain that makes them ideal for pounding into fufu – to get that sticky viscous consistency that fufu demands – however as those complex carbohydrates are very slowly released its colouring and ripeness develop, as it changes through yellow to black.

By the time the plantain has become overripe (black), the starches have converted to sucrose, giving it that natural super sweetness.

So in this section we'll explore just a handful of the many ways of cooking plantain during its life cycle, from baked to boiled and – my favourite and most delicious version – FRIED!

★ This dish takes of advantage of the nutrient-packed green plantain at the beginning of the long life of the fruit. It's usually served with kontomire (see Kontomire & Apem Stew, page 95) and handily doubles as cutlery, since you can use it like a spoon to scoop up your stew, or just chomp on it like a banana after dipping it into the sauce!

SERVES 4
AS A SIDE

Apem

½ **teaspoon** cooking salt

4 green plantains

Put a saucepan of water on to the boil and add the salt.

Peel your plantains by cutting the tips off each end and removing the skin with your fingers, leaving the plantain whole – the high starch level in unripe plantain makes it quite tough to peel, so you'll need to apply some pressure and leverage.

Add the whole plantains to the boiling water and cook for 10–15 minutes – you want the plantain to be firm on the outside but soft inside, so test with a fork.

Once ready, drain the plantains and plunge into cold water to make sure they remain firm. Drain again before serving.

Simple Fried Plantain

★ This is the simplest fried plantain recipe by far – no frills or fuss. It relies purely on the plantain being ripe, but not overripe, to achieve that naturally sweet flavour and al dente bite. So in this case the plantain should be deep yellow all over with no signs of green at all – and starting to be mottled black is even better!

For that true taste of Ghana, a sustainable palm oil is the best choice here, although groundnut oil works really well, too, and sunflower or vegetable oil are acceptable alternatives.

Because fried plantains are so moreish, I always allow at least one plantain per person as a side dish, as everyone always wants more; simply up the quantity according to the number of guests you have for dinner and how greedy they are!

4 ripe plantains

sustainable palm oil or groundnut oil, for shallow-frying

1 red chilli of your choice, deseeded and diced, to garnish (optional)

Using a sharp knife, peel the plantains by cutting the tips off each end and slicing through the skin lengthways (avoid cutting into the flesh), then use your hands to remove the skin. Remove any stringy fibres you may find.

I like to cut the plantains in half lengthways and then into several pieces on the diagonal – skinny (1cm/½-inch) pieces or chunky (2–3cm/¾–1¼-inch) pieces work equally well, but simply adjust the quantity of oil and frying time according to the thickness.

Pour enough oil into a large frying pan to cover the base by a depth of 5mm–1cm (¼–½ inch) – you don't need to submerge the plantain in oil – and heat over a medium–high heat.

Fry the pieces of plantain, in batches, by gently lowering each piece into the hot oil with tongs – be careful not to overcrowd the pan so that you can turn them easily and avoid the oil splattering. They should start to turn golden pretty quickly, and when you can see a golden brown crust forming at the edges of the plantain pieces, gently turn them over and cook until well browned on the other side. Remove from the pan and drain on kitchen paper, keeping the cooked plantain warm while you fry the rest.

Eat the plantain pieces on their own, garnished with fresh chilli if liked, or serve warm with a stew – these are especially good with Red Red Stew (see page 116) and any dish containing Peanut Sauce (see page 249).

★ I wrote earlier about the long life of a plantain, and this recipe is great for using up fruits that have turned black all over and may even be starting to become mouldy – yes, mouldy! This may be the end of the life cycle, but it also means that the plantain has reached its most fully ripened and sweetest state, and you can probably buy five or six such plantains for £1 from the grocer – result! This is super-simple, fast and hands-down delicious.

Tatale
Plantain Pancakes

4 overripe plantains

2 onions, roughly chopped

½ Scotch Bonnet chilli, deseeded and chopped

2.5cm (1-inch) piece fresh root ginger, grated (unpeeled if organic)

¾ teaspoon ground hot pepper, or substitute cayenne pepper

sea salt, to taste

280g (10oz) rice flour, as needed

2 tablespoons sustainable palm oil or carotene oil, for shallow-frying

Peel the plantains, chop into bite-sized chunks and throw into a blender or food processor along with the onions, chilli, ginger, ground pepper and sea salt to taste and blend together until well combined but still with some texture, adding the rice flour as needed to achieve a consistency akin to drop scone batter. If you don't have a blender or food processor, mash the ingredients together well in a bowl – it doesn't need to be a super-smooth mixture, and it's quite nice to have small chunks of plantain in it.

Heat 1 tablespoon of the oil in a nonstick frying pan over a medium-high heat and, once hot, add 1 tablespoon of the plantain mixture to the pan. Using the back of the spoon or a palette knife, gently spread the mixture into a pancake – I have found the ideal thickness to be 1cm (½ inch) and about 4cm (1½ inches) in diameter. Repeat with more of the plantain mixture, depending on how many pancakes your pan will accommodate.

When the pancakes begin to bubble a little and start browning at the edges, use a palette knife to gently turn them over. Fry for a few minutes on the other side. Remove from the pan and repeat with the remaining plantain mixture, keeping the cooked pancakes hot while you fry the rest. Serve hot or warm.

→ **TIP** This is a dish that can be made with nearly ripe or overripe plantain and the consistency will depend on exactly how ripe the plantain is — if using super-ripe plantain you may need to add cornflour or rice flour to create the correct drop scone consistency — these are quite delicate pancakes, not fluffy and big like buttermilk pancakes, so require a gentle hand when turning to avoid splitting the batter mix.

Kelewele
Spiced Plantain

★ When out walking in Kaneshie, the town in Ghana where my grandmother lives, in the hot dusk of the evening among the clatter and chaos of life, amid the sound of tro-tro (share taxi) drivers shouting out their destinations to attract fares, it's hard to avoid the soothing and dominant, sweet and spicy aroma of spiced ginger cooking on sweet plantain that emanates from almost every street. Hard to avoid and nigh on impossible to resist.

This is kelewele (pronounced 'kaylay-waylay'), a simple and quick side dish of spiced and fried plantain, and a common snack available from roadside chop bars and street-food vendors across Ghana.

There are a few different recipes out there for this dish and it goes by various names in different parts of West Africa, but the principle is the same – ripe plantain cooked in fresh spices. It can be as simple as marinating the plantain in a mix of very finely chopped onion, grated fresh root ginger, chilli flakes and salt. I also like to make a sweet aromatic version using nutmeg, cinnamon and cloves, which combines the best of what I've tasted on the streets of Accra.

→ **TIP** *The secret to a good fried plantain is to use fruit at the correct stage of ripeness. Here, this is when the plantain is mottled black but still yellow and firm, and as fleshy as the skin on the inside of your wrist.*

1 heaped tablespoon Kelewele Dry Spice Mix (see page 245)

1 small red onion, grated

5cm (2-inch) piece fresh root ginger, grated (unpeeled if organic)

pinch of sea salt

500ml–1 litre (18fl oz–1¾ pints) coconut oil for deep-frying, plus **2 tablespoons** for marinating, or substitute vegetable oil

4–6 ripe plantains (see Tip, below left)

handful of roasted peanuts, crushed, to garnish (optional)

Mix the dry spice mix with the onion, ginger, sea salt and the 2 tablespoons oil in a bowl.

Using a sharp knife, peel the plantains by cutting the tips off each end and slicing through the skin lengthways (avoid cutting into the flesh), then use your hands to remove the skin.

Cut the plantains in half lengthways into 2 long pieces. Usually the plantain is then diced into 2cm (¾-inch) squares or bite-sized chunks, but I like to make chunky plantain chips with this spice mix, so I cut the plantain in half across the middle, making 4 pieces, and then each piece in half lengthways again to end up with 8 evenly sized chunky chips from each plantain. This way, the plantain chips will cook evenly and quickly without burning.

Coat the plantain chips in the spice mix and leave to stand at room temperature for at least 20 minutes. You can also cover the bowl with clingfilm and place in the fridge for longer to soak up the marinade until you're ready to cook.

Heat the oil for deep-frying in a deep-fat fryer (the safest option) or heavy-based, deep saucepan filled to just under half the depth of the pan to 180–190°C (350–375°F) or until a cube of bread browns in 30 seconds. Fry the plantain chips, in batches, until they float to the surface and are evenly golden in colour – you should have a crispy spiced outside and sweet soft inside. Remove from the oil and drain on kitchen paper, keeping the cooked chips hot while you fry the rest. Alternatively, preheat the oven to 180°C (350°F), Gas Mark 4. Spread the coated plantain chips out on a baking tray and bake for about 20 minutes until golden on the outside and tender inside. Serve hot.

With or without the garnish of crushed roasted peanuts, this makes a great appetizer, snack or side for both meat and veggie dishes!

★ So you managed to get your five or six overripe plantains for £1 and have sampled Tatale (*see page 43*), but have a couple left over. This recipe is another perfect use for those super-sweet plantains, and while very similar to tatale, it has its own nuanced texture and flavour that comes from the style of cooking.

If you're lucky enough to own an asanka pot, this is where it comes into its own. The asanka is a traditional mortar and pestle, and I love the action of grinding spices and mixes in one of these. It's ideal for extracting all the natural flavours and oils from ingredients, whereas sometimes a blender or food processor can destroy some of that natural goodness and taste.

Krakro/Kaklo
Spicy Plantain Balls

3 overripe plantains

1 small onion, finely grated

2.5cm (1-inch) piece fresh root ginger, grated (unpeeled if organic)

1 red Scotch Bonnet chilli, deseeded and finely diced (you can adjust the heat by using less fresh chilli or ½ teaspoon dried chilli flakes)

1 teaspoon sea salt

½ teaspoon ground hot pepper, or substitute cayenne pepper (optional)

120ml (4fl oz) water

3 tablespoons plain flour or cornflour

500ml–1 litre (18fl oz–1¾ pints) vegetable oil, for deep-frying

1 spring onion, finely sliced, to garnish (optional)

Using a sharp knife, peel the plantains by cutting the tips off each end and slicing through the skin lengthways (avoid cutting into the flesh), then use your hands to remove the skin. Then either pound them with a wooden spoon in a bowl or whizz in a blender or food processor.

Add the onion, ginger, Scotch Bonnet, sea salt, chilli powder (if using) and about one-third of the measured water along with 2 tablespoons of the flour or cornflour and stir well. If the mixture is too wet, add a little more flour or cornflour; if it seems too dry, add a little more water. You're aiming for a consistency akin to drop scone batter as with Tatale, not a runny mixture.

Leave the mixture to rest at room temperature for 20–30 minutes.

Heat the oil for deep-frying in a deep-fat fryer (the safest option) or heavy-based, deep saucepan filled to just under half the depth of the pan to 160–170°C (325–340°F) – as very ripe plantains contain a high sugar content, they will burn easily, so make sure that the temperature isn't higher than this. Using a wooden spoon, scoop up spoonfuls of the mixture, drop into the hot oil and deep-fry, in batches, for 3–4 minutes until golden and crisp. Remove from the oil and drain well on kitchen paper, keeping the cooked balls hot while you fry the rest. Serve hot, sprinkled with sliced spring onion if liked.

Krakro/Kaklo

Kelewele

Simple Fried Plantain

Tatale

Apem

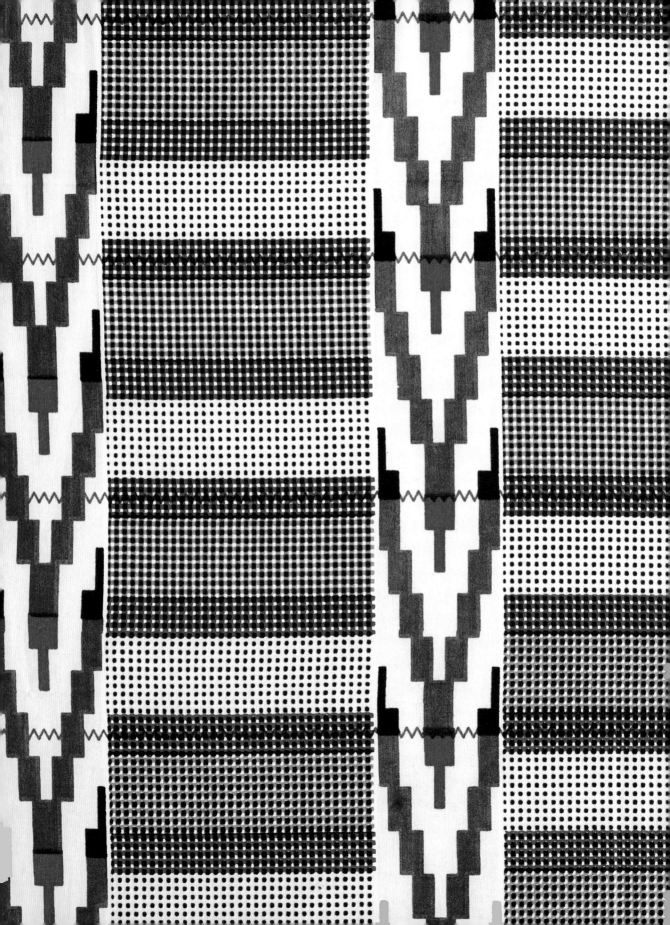

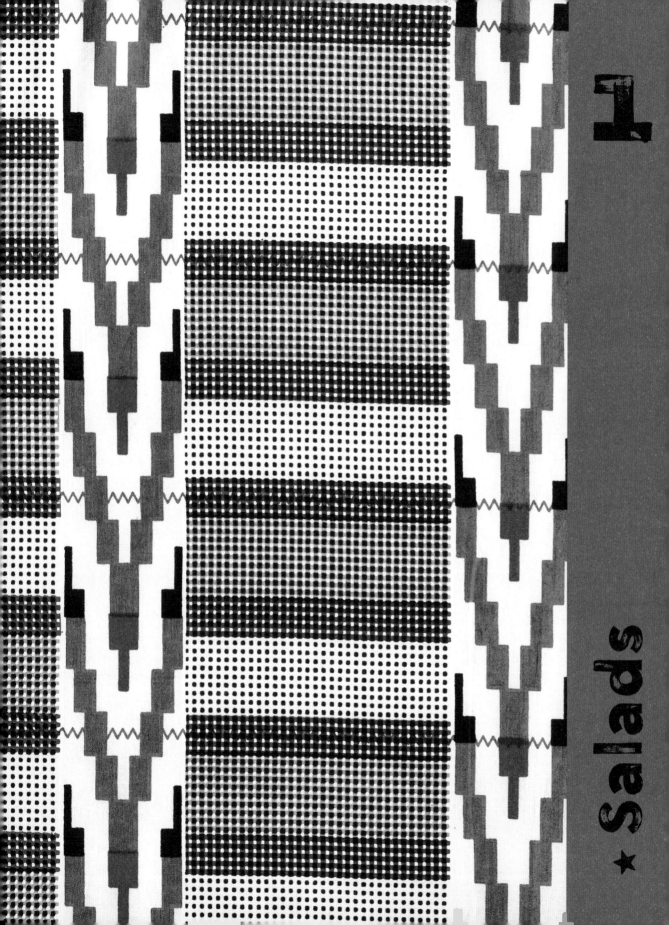

★ Salads

GHANA GO HOME:
A Soundtrack to Cook to

★ When you want the feeling of being back at home in Ghana, apart from the food itself, having a soundtrack to bring to mind the sights and sounds of everyday Ghanaian life and culture can transform the cooking process from an arduous task into a party in the kitchen. And let's face it, all parties end up in the kitchen anyway!

So settle into this backing track of Ghanaian High-life and Afro-beat to sway your way through cooking and dining, and maybe even bust some Azonto dance moves around the kitchen as you go.

Zoe's Ghana Kitchen playlist is available for subscription on Spotify, with music compiled by DJ Aries. (Also, see my Soundtrack to Eat to on page 240).

	Artist	Track	Album	Song Length
1	E T Mensah	*Ghana-Guinea-Mali*	Day By Day	2.45
2	C K Mann	*Okuan Tsentsen Awar*	Ghana Funk	6.44
3	Ebo Taylor	*Nga Nga*	Love & Death	5.24
4	Ebo Taylor	*African Woman*	Love & Death	7.04
5	Gyedu-Blay Ambolley	*Afrika Yie*	Sekunde	6.57
6	Kwashibu Area Band	*Gyae Su*	Pat Thomas & Kwashibu Area Band	4.12
7	Kwashibu Area Band	*Amaehu*	Pat Thomas & Kwashibu Area Band	5.4
8	Daddy Lumba	*Nana Addo*	Appietus in the Mix, Vol.1	3.39
9	R2Bees	*Odo*	Refuse To Be Broke	3.51
10	Jay Ghartey	*My Lady*	My Lady	4.27
11	Bisa Kdei	*Mansa*	Break Through	4.06
12	Keche	*Diabetes*	Best of Keche	3.55
13	R2Bees	*Lobi*	Lobi	3.11
14	Sarkodie, Bisa Kdei	*Chingam*	Chingam	3.34
15	DJ Stretch	*Adonai Remix*	Adonai Remix	4.48
16	Yaa Pono, Eddy Kay	*Atinga*	Atinga	4.18
17	Mr Eazi, JuLS	*Skintight*	Skintight	3.25
18	Mr Eazi, JuLS	*Shitor*	Shitor	3.5
19	M3NSA	*No One Knows*	No.1 Mango Street	3.29
20	JuLS, M3NSA, PappyKojo	*Gidigidi*	Gidigidi	3.55
21	Efya	*Release*	Janesis	3.37
22	Efya	*Make I Love You*	Janesis	2.52
23	EL	*Auntie Martha*	Something Else	4.26
24	EL	*Mame Wossop*	Something Else	2.55
25	Joey B, Sarkodie	*Tonga*	Tonga	3.22
26	Shatta Wale	*Everybody Like My Ting*	Answers	2.39
27	Samini, Joey B, PappyKojo	*Zingolo*	Breaking News	3.53

Ghana Salad

★ This is basically the mother of all salads with everything but the kitchen sink thrown in – a hugely substantial feast of colour, texture and flavour. I have to point out that this is normally not a very healthy salad with its lashings of mayonnaise and/ or Marie Rose sauce, but I've come up with a recipe that focuses on fresh ingredients rather than the canned ones commonly used (canned baked varieties are a favourite in Ghana!) while sticking to the original formula.

200g (7oz) whole fresh sardines, scaled, gutted and washed, or substitute canned

200g (7oz) fresh tuna steak, or substitute canned

1 round Iceberg lettuce, shredded

4 tomatoes, deseeded and sliced

2 red onions, finely sliced

175g (6oz) green beans, topped and tailed, sliced and steamed, then chilled

100g (3½oz) fresh garden peas, lightly blanched, then drained and chilled

200g (7oz) drained good-quality canned organic cannellini beans, chilled

150g (5½oz) smoked salmon, cut into strips, or substitute flaked canned salmon

1 teaspoon sea salt

1 teaspoon coarsely ground black pepper

4–6 large eggs, soft-boiled, shelled and quartered

salad cream or mayonnaise, to taste

Preheat the grill to medium. Place the sardines and tuna steak on the grill rack and grill for 10–15 minutes, turning halfway through the cooking time. Leave to cool, then chill in the fridge before adding to the salad.

Place the lettuce, tomatoes and onions in a large bowl, then add the green beans, peas, cannellini beans and smoked salmon.

Flake the grilled tuna and add to the salad, season with the sea salt and black pepper and mix together carefully. Add the grilled sardines and garnish with the soft-boiled egg quarters.

Cover and chill before serving. When ready to serve, dress with salad cream or mayonnaise to taste and serve with warm toasted baguette, ciabatta or hard dough bread.

→ **TIPS** I used to drown my Ghana Salad in salad cream — guilty pleasures — but if you want a healthier option, make a vinaigrette of 3 parts olive oil to 1 part balsamic vinegar and season with sea salt and black pepper, then add to the salad before serving.

Hard dough bread (also known as 'butter bread') is a white loaf that is slightly sweet. It can be bought sliced or unsliced.

★ Cooked well, yam has a wonderful fluffy bite to it and it's as versatile as any potato, making it a great alternative – besides boiling it as here, you can fry it, mash it or prepare it gratin style. This makes a great barbecue side with Suya Goat Kebabs, Suya Beef Kebabs and Jamestown Grilled Prawns (see pages 124, 126 and 70), or a late summer salad.

Warm Yam Salad

cooking salt

2 Romano peppers

½ **tablespoon** rapeseed oil or olive oil

pinch of sea salt

coarsely ground black pepper, to season

350–400g (12–14oz) yam

1 red onion, sliced

2 spring onions, finely chopped

1 avocado, stoned, peeled and chopped into chunks

1 **teaspoon** ground hot pepper, or substitute cayenne pepper

100–120g (3½–4¼oz) salted fish, steamed and flaked

sustainable palm oil or carotene oil, for drizzling

Preheat the oven to 180°C (350°F), Gas Mark 4 and line a baking tray with greaseproof paper. Put a saucepan of salted water on to boil.

Slice each pepper lengthways into 4 strips, discarding the seeds. Lay the strips out on the lined tray, drizzle with the rapeseed or olive oil and season with the sea salt and black pepper. Roast for 15–20 minutes.

While the peppers are roasting, prepare the yam. Have a bowl or pan of water ready before you start, as you'll need to put each peeled yam piece straight into water as you go to prevent them oxidizing and turning brown. Slice the yam into discs 1cm (½ inch) thick and then peel as if peeling an apple. Chop each disc into 2.5cm (1-inch) cubes, then rinse thoroughly in cold water to remove the starch.

Add the yam chunks to the salted boiling water and cook for 12–15 minutes until just fork tender. Drain well and leave in a bowl for the steam to rise, then cover with a plate or clean cloth.

Remove the peppers from the oven and leave them to cool slightly before cutting into slightly smaller strips on the diagonal.

Add all the remaining ingredients except the oil, along with the roasted peppers, to the yam bowl and toss together gently. Drizzle with palm or carotene oil and serve warm.

→ **TIP** You can turn this dish vegan by simply omitting the fish, or vary it by using smoked instead of salted fish, such as smoked mackerel.

★ When it comes to papaya, with its somewhat affectionate-sounding alternative name of pawpaw, most people think of Thai and East Asian food, but Ghana has it in abundance, along with avocados, so it seems only fitting to throw these luscious fruits together in a salad. Chuck in a mango, drizzle with some fresh ginger dressing and you have the perfect summer party salad.

SERVES 4 AS A MAIN
SERVES 6 AS A SIDE

Avocado, Papaya & Ginger Salad

1 ripe papaya, deseeded, peeled and cubed

1 ripe mango, stoned, peeled and cubed

2 ripe avocados, stoned, peeled and cubed

150g (5½oz) cherry or baby plum tomatoes, halved (optional)

1 red onion, finely sliced

1 cucumber, deseeded and sliced into rounds

50g (1¾oz) or ½ bunch of coriander, chopped

50-75g (1¾-2¾oz) salted roasted peanuts, to garnish (optional)

DRESSING

2.5cm (1-inch) piece fresh root ginger, finely grated (unpeeled if organic)

½ teaspoon cayenne pepper (optional)

1 teaspoon soft light brown sugar

½ teaspoon wholegrain mustard (optional)

about 1½ tablespoons extra virgin olive oil

1 tablespoon lemon juice

1 tablespoon rice vinegar, or substitute cider vinegar

sea salt and coarsely ground black pepper, to taste

Place all the dressing ingredients in a screw-top jar with a tight-fitting lid, seal with the lid and shake well to combine. You can then store the dressing for later – it should keep for up to 5 days in the fridge – or use straight away.

Add all the prepared fresh ingredients to a salad bowl and drizzle over the dressing. Garnish with the crushed peanuts, if using.

→ **TIP** *This makes a great side with Jamestown Grilled Prawns (see page 70) or any other seafood dishes, especially Fante Fried Fish, Fried Squid or Pan-fried Tilapia Fillets (see pages 76, 88 and 82).*

★ The garden egg often suffers the same fate as okra – being plonked into stews, thereby obliterating its flavour. But despite the fact that it looks very unlike the purple aubergine – often white, it closely resembles a boiled egg – it can be cooked in any of the many ways that you can cook regular aubergine including steaming, grilling, making into crisps or roasting as here. This super-healthy salad makes a delicious brunch or lunch.

SERVES 2 AS A MAIN
SERVES 4 AS A SIDE

Garden Egg & Quinoa Salad

5-6 garden eggs (African aubergines), trimmed and quartered

1 **teaspoon** dried chilli flakes

1 garlic clove, very finely chopped

3 **tablespoons** rapeseed oil

sea salt and freshly ground black pepper

200g (7oz) quinoa

400ml (14fl oz) warm water

pinch of cooking salt

½ **head** of broccoli, broken into bite-sized pieces, or use Tenderstem broccoli spears

1 red onion, finely sliced

1 **tablespoon** chopped coriander

2 **tablespoons** lemon juice

50g (1¾oz) feta cheese, crumbled

Preheat the oven to 200°C (400°F), Gas Mark 6. Line a baking tray with greaseproof paper.

Put the garden egg quarters in a bowl, add the chilli flakes, garlic, 1 tablespoon of the oil and sea salt and black pepper and toss together, making sure that each garden quarter is evenly coated.

Spread the garden egg quarters out on the lined baking tray and roast for about 15 minutes, turning them halfway through the cooking time – they should take on a lovely golden hue and slight crispness around the edges.

Meanwhile, prepare the quinoa. Put the quinoa in a saucepan, add the measured warm water and cooking salt and bring to the boil, then reduce the heat and simmer for 15 minutes or until the water has been absorbed.

While the quinoa is simmering, steam the broccoli – for convenience, you can place it in a metal colander or sieve, set it over the quinoa pan, cover and steam until al dente.

Once the broccoli and the quinoa are cooked, remove from the heat and leave to cool.

Mix the onion, coriander and lemon juice together gently in a bowl and season to taste with sea salt and black pepper. Add the roasted garden egg and steamed broccoli and stir through, then add the quinoa and toss to mix. Finally, scatter the feta on top.

Mango & Pineapple Salad

★ It has to be said that Ghanaians aren't big on salads as a mainstay of their diet, but there are plenty of wonderful fresh ingredients that can be combined to make them, so there is every opportunity to get inventive. Check out this super-simple and healthy pairing of ripe mango and pineapple with fruit juices.

50ml (2fl oz) fresh orange juice

2 tablespoons apple juice

juice of 1 lemon

2 ripe mangoes, stoned, peeled and cubed

½ fresh pineapple, peeled, cored and cubed, or substitute **200–300g/7–10½oz** canned pineapple chunks if fresh is unavailable

½ cucumber, sliced (optional)

200–250g (7–9oz) rocket

pinch of sea salt

50g (1¾oz) Spiced Cashews (see page 208), crushed or whole

Mix the fruit juices together and add to the prepared mangoes and pineapple in a bowl.

If using the cucumber, cut it in half lengthways and use a teaspoon to scoop out the seeds, then slice into whatever shapes you prefer – I like simple half moons.

Remove the fruit chunks from the bowl, reserving the excess juices, and gently toss with the rocket and cucumber in a separate bowl. Drizzle a little of the reserved fruit juices over the salad and add the sea salt.

Garnish with the spiced cashews and serve on a side plate alongside Fried Barracuda, Lamb Palaver or goat Kontomire Froe (see recipes on pages 77, 136 and 130 – use goat meat in place of beef for the Kontomire Froe).

★ I'm guessing that almost everyone who loves food has had a Caesar salad in their lifetime, and there is no denying that it's a pretty surefire formula for a very tasty dish. But how about putting a little extra bang into that favourite standard with some great Ghanaian ingredients?

Ghana-fied Caesar Salad

2 boneless, skinless chicken breasts, cut into strips

1 heaped tablespoon Jollof Dry Spice Mix (see page 244)

1 tablespoon rapeseed oil

5–6 dried smoked herring, soaked in boiling water for 30 minutes, or substitute 1 can of anchovy fillets

1 large Cos (Romaine) lettuce, leaves separated and roughly chopped or torn into large pieces

1 tablespoon sustainable palm oil or carotene oil, for drizzling (optional)

1 teaspoon each of sea salt and ground black pepper, to taste

CROUTONS

4 thick slices of hard dough bread, or substitute crusty white bread

4 tablespoons rapeseed oil or olive oil

1 teaspoon sea salt

DRESSING

50g (1¾oz) Parmesan or Grana Padano cheese, shaved or grated

5 tablespoons Shito Mayo (see page 231)

1 garlic clove, very finely chopped

1 tablespoon white wine vinegar

1 tablespoon rapeseed oil or olive oil

sea salt, to taste

First make the croutons. Preheat the oven to 180°C (350°F), Gas Mark 4. Cut your slices of bread into 2–3cm (¾–1¼-inch) cubes. Spread over a baking sheet or tray. Sprinkle over the oil and sea salt, then toss together to coat the bread cubes. Bake for 7–8 minutes, turning the croutons halfway through the cooking time so that they brown evenly. Remove from the oven and set aside.

Season the chicken strips with the jollof dry spice mix in a bowl, then add the rapeseed oil and toss to coat.

Heat a frying pan or preheat the grill to medium heat. Add the chicken strips to the pan or place on a baking tray under the grill and fry or grill for about 4 minutes on each side or until the juices run clear when pierced with a knife. Set aside.

Drain the smoked herring (or anchovy fillets) and use a fork to break up into smaller pieces.

For the dressing, mix half the cheese with the shito mayo, garlic and vinegar in a bowl. Loosen with the oil and season to taste with sea salt.

Put the lettuce in a large bowl and scatter the chicken strips among the leaves with half the croutons. Add half the dressing and toss together lightly. Top with the remaining chicken strips, croutons and pieces of smoked herring, then drizzle with the remaining dressing. Sprinkle the remaining cheese on top and, for a dash of extra colour and Ghanaian flavour, drizzle the palm oil across the salad. Season to taste with salt and pepper and serve straight away.

★ There are so many uses for plantain and this makes an exciting change from the usual sort of side salad. For ripe plantains, look for those that are mostly yellow but flecked with black dots and easy to squeeze. Ripe plantains cook faster than green and will be much sweeter, too. Boiling them in their skins also intensifies their flavour.

Plantain Salad

2 very ripe plantains

pinch of cooking salt

500g (1lb 2oz) rocket or corn salad

1 small green pepper, cored, deseeded and sliced very finely

1 small cucumber, peeled, cored, deseeded and diced

1 small Scotch Bonnet chilli, deseeded and diced

50ml (2fl oz) rapeseed oil or extra virgin olive oil

2 tablespoons lime juice

1 teaspoon cumin seeds, toasted and roughly crushed

½ teaspoon sea salt, or to taste

¼ teaspoon freshly ground black pepper

soft light brown sugar, to taste

chopped coriander leaves, to garnish

Wash the plantains, then, using a sharp knife, cut the tips off each end. Make a slit in the skin along the length of each plantain, but do not peel – this will make the skin easier to remove once cooked. Cut into 3 or 4 pieces.

Place the plantains in a saucepan with enough water to cover and the cooking salt and bring to the boil, then reduce the heat and simmer for 10–15 minutes or until the plantains are soft enough to allow a fork or tip of a sharp knife to pass through them with ease.

Drain the plantains and leave to cool, then remove the skin.

Toss the salad leaves, green pepper, cucumber and chilli together in a salad bowl. Whisk the oil, lime juice, cumin, sea salt, black pepper and sugar to taste together, then add to the salad with the plantains and toss to coat. Garnish with chopped coriander and serve.

★ Pulses are a mainstay of Ghanaian cooking. Usually forming the basis of stews, they can also be a great addition to boost a simple salad.

Three Bean Salad

3 × 400g (14oz) cans organic mixed beans, such as pinto, black-eyed and cannellini

1 Spanish or red onion, finely diced

1 tablespoon chopped coriander

1 Scotch Bonnet chilli, deseeded and diced

2 garlic cloves, very finely chopped

½ teaspoon sea salt

½ teaspoon freshly ground black pepper

juice of 1 lime

2 tablespoons olive oil

1 teaspoon soft dark brown sugar

1 teaspoon clear honey

Drain the cans of beans, rinse and drain again, then set aside.

Mix all the remaining ingredients together thoroughly in a large salad bowl, then add the drained beans and toss to mix.

Cover the bowl with clingfilm and chill in the fridge for 1 hour before serving.

★ Spice up your life with this crunchy version of spicy slaw – the secret weapon is in the title and it packs a punch.

AS A SIDE

Scotch Bonnet Coleslaw

¼ white cabbage, sliced

¼ small red cabbage, sliced

2–3 carrots, peeled (if not organic) and grated

2 red apples, cored and finely sliced

1 large red Scotch Bonnet, deseeded and diced

1 teaspoon cayenne pepper

75g or 3 tablespoons mayonnaise (see Tip, below)

1 teaspoon sea salt

1 teaspoon freshly ground black pepper

juice of 2 lemons

Mix the cabbages, carrots, apples, chilli and cayenne pepper together in a bowl.

Add the mayo, sea salt, black pepper and lemon juice, and toss together to coat the vegetables and apples evenly in the dressing and seasoning.

→ TIP Instead of using shop-bought mayonnaise, make your own spicy mayo by following the recipe for Shito Mayo on page 231 but omitting the shito.

★ Fish & Seafood

2

★ Grains of paradise make a great addition to any fish marinade, especially if roasted before grinding, as their nutty flavour enhances rather than overpowers delicately flavoured fish such as cod. This recipe is ideal for a super-fast brunch.

Pan-roasted Cod Seasoned with Grains of Paradise

½ **teaspoon** grains of paradise

450g (1lb) cod fillet, cut into 2 pieces

sea salt, to season

1 tablespoon groundnut oil

extra virgin olive oil, for sprinkling

1 lemon, cut into wedges, to serve

chopped parsley, to garnish

Preheat the oven to 200°C (400°F), Gas Mark 6.

Toast the grains of paradise in a dry ovenproof frying pan over a medium-high heat, then leave to cool. Coarsely grind with a mortar and pestle.

Season the cod on both sides with sea salt and a pinch of the ground grains of paradise.

Return the frying pan to a medium heat, add the groundnut oil and heat. Add the cod to the centre of the pan and sauté for 2–3 minutes until crisped and brown, then gently turn over and sauté the other side for 1 minute.

Transfer the pan to the oven to finish cooking for 2–3 minutes, depending on the thickness of the fish. Remove from the oven and place on serving plates.

Drizzle with olive oil and sprinkle the remaining ground grains of paradise on top. Squeeze a little lemon juice over the fish, scatter with chopped parsley and serve with lemon wedges on the side.

Jamestown Grilled Prawns

★ Grilling over charcoal is the favoured way to cook most fish and seafood in Ghana – especially along the Accra coastline where there is an abundance of fresh seafood, and up into the region alongside Lake Volta.

This recipe is inspired by my experience in Jamestown, Accra, where I watched the local fisherman hauling in their catches (see My Ghana Story Part 3; page 166).

1kg (2lb 4oz) uncooked king prawns or tiger prawns

4 tablespoons coconut oil

1 onion, finely shredded or grated

grated **zest and juice of 2** lemons

2 tablespoons chopped thyme

1 heaped teaspoon ground ginger, or grated fresh root ginger

1 teaspoon grated garlic

2 teaspoons ground hot pepper, or substitute cayenne pepper

1 heaped teaspoon dried ground prawn/shrimp powder

1 teaspoon sea salt

Wash the prawns and remove the heads but leave the shells on for a more dramatic presentation. Butterfly the prawns so that you create a greater surface area for your seasoning: using a sharp knife, score down the belly and open out. This will also enable you to de-vein the prawns. Rinse thoroughly and pat dry. You can ask your fishmonger to prepare the prawns for you, if you prefer.

Put 2 tablespoons of the coconut oil in a bowl with all the remaining ingredients and mix well. Add the prepared prawns and gently turn to coat them all over with the marinade. If you have time, cover the bowl with clingfilm and leave in the fridge for 30 minutes to soak up the marinade while you light your charcoal barbecue and the coals have burnt down until covered in a grey ash (see Tips, left). Alternatively, preheat a gas barbecue to medium-high.

Once the barbecue is ready for cooking, thread the prawns on to skewers (see Tips, left).

Brush the barbecue grill well with some of the reserved coconut oil and also drizzle the oil over the skewers, coating each side. Add the skewers to the grill and cook for 3–4 minutes on each side.

Serve with a selection of dips and salsas, such as Green Kpakpo Shito Salsa, Mango and Pineapple Salad and plain boiled or Coconut Rice (see pages 231, 58 and 172).

➔ **TIPS** *Remember to preheat a charcoal barbecue about 30 minutes before you want to start cooking.*

If you are using bamboo skewers, put them in water to soak for 1 hour to prevent them burning on the barbecue.

Garden Egg Stew with Tilapia

★ This is one of the most popular stews in Ghana. The common habit of plonking the slightly bitter garden egg (African aubergine) into stews in the same way as potatoes, which ordinarily diminishes its flavour and texture through overcooking, actually works to its advantage here. It results in a wonderfully rich dish with deep, intense flavours.

1–2 large fresh tilapia, filleted, each cut into 3 pieces

sea salt

1 tablespoon ground grains of paradise, or substitute
1 tablespoon ground mace

10 large garden eggs (African aubergines), trimmed and halved

150ml (5fl oz) sustainable palm oil or carotene oil

2 large onions, diced

1 tablespoon ground hot pepper, or substitute cayenne pepper

1 teaspoon ground nutmeg

2 teaspoons dried ground prawn/shrimp powder (optional)

6–8 large tomatoes

2 Scotch Bonnet chillies, pierced, and or/**a handful** of whole green kpakpo shito (cherry) chillies

1 small fresh ginger root, grated (unpeeled if organic)

150ml (5fl oz) water

Place the tilapia pieces in a dish and season with sea salt and the grains of paradise, then cover with clingfilm and leave to marinate in the fridge for 1 hour.

Meanwhile, cook the garden eggs in a saucepan of boiling water for 10–15 minutes until they become transparent and the skin begins to come away. Drain, leave to cool and then peel off the skins. Using a fork, mash into a rough paste and set aside.

Heat the palm oil in a large, heavy-based saucepan, add the onions and fry for 5 minutes. Add the ground hot pepper, nutmeg and prawn/shrimp powder and leave to cook for 3 minutes.

Put the tomatoes in a blender or food processor and blend to a purée, then add to the pan of frying onions with the chillies, ginger and 100ml (3½fl oz) of the measured water and cook, stirring regularly, for about 20 minutes.

Stir the mashed garden eggs into the stew, then add the remaining 50ml (1½fl oz) water, stir through and bring to just below boiling point. Add the tilapia, then reduce the heat and leave the stew to simmer gently, stirring occasionally, for a further 15–20 minutes.

Check the seasoning and add sea salt to taste if required. Serve immediately with your choice of side dish: Fufu, Savoury Fried Yam or Simple Fried Plantain (see pages 173, 33 and 42).

➔ **TIPS** *Tilapia is now widely farmed in the West, so it's readily available to buy fresh, either whole or in fillets.*

You can also chop the garden egg so that you don't have to boil it and remove the skins — just add to the stew after the blended tomatoes.

★ This is such a simple, fresh and healthy recipe – the perfect summer dish. Even the butter has been made beneficial to health by the addition of mineral- and vitamin-packed baobab powder (*see page 24*).

SERVES 4

Pan-fried Prawns in Spiced Baobab Butter

1 teaspoon Spiced Baobab Butter (see page 232)

500g (1lb 2oz) uncooked peeled and deveined prawns

sprig of coriander, or sliced chilli of your choice, to serve

Heat a frying pan over a medium heat. Add the butter to the pan and heat until foaming. Add the prawns and stir-fry for a few minutes until they turn pink all over and are cooked through.

Thread the prawns on to skewers and serve on a bed of Coconut Rice (see page 172), garnished with the coriander sprig or chilli, with a side of spinach or spring greens sautéed in a little coconut oil.

★ Tilapia is the most common freshwater fish in Ghana, its meaty flesh providing a substantial meal. This recipe is based on a very traditional style of cooking tilapia that can be found all across Ghana. But if the idea of looking your dinner in the eye is intimidating, you can use tilapia fillets instead.

Whole Grilled Tilapia

2 fresh tilapia, scaled, gutted and washed

lime wedges

MARINADE

1 white onion, grated

1 tablespoon rapeseed oil

5cm (2-inch) piece fresh root ginger, grated (unpeeled if organic)

1 garlic clove, very finely chopped

2 green kpakpo shito (cherry) chillies, deseeded and finely diced, or substitute green habanero chillies

juice of 1 lime

2 tablespoons ground grains of paradise, or substitute ½ teaspoon ground mace or nutmeg

½ teaspoon dried chilli flakes

½ teaspoon ground hot pepper, or substitute cayenne pepper

sea salt and freshly ground pepper, to taste

Using a sharp cook's knife, remove the gill coverings and hard fins from the tilapia – this is a messy job, so it's worth asking your fishmonger to do it for you. Carefully cut 3 evenly spaced diagonal slashes into either side of the fish – tilapia skin is very thick, so you'll need a firm, steady hand. Place the prepared fish in a dish.

Mix all the ingredients for the marinade together in a bowl or place in a blender or food processor and blend to a smooth paste.

Pour the marinade over the fish, reserving a small amount for basting, and rub into the slashes and inside the cavity of each fish. Cover the dish with clingfilm and leave the fish to marinate in the fridge for at least 1 hour, preferably overnight.

Remove from the fridge a few minutes before you're ready to cook and preheat the grill to medium-high. Place the fish on a baking tray lined with foil and cook under the grill for 25 minutes (add an extra 3–5 minutes if the fish are particularly large or thick) until nicely browned and cooked through, turning and basting with the reserved marinade halfway through the cooking time.

Serve with Green Kpakpo Shito Salsa and Banku (see pages 231 and 169) or plain boiled rice, along with lime wedges for squeezing over.

Fante-Fante
Fante Fish Soup

★ My grandmother comes from the Fante coastal region of Elmina, a world away from downtown Accra's shiny new buildings and the wide-paved roads of Osu. These people love seafood and take fish seriously. The hundreds of small fishing boats crammed together in the harbour remind me of commuters on a packed train, sterns elbowing each other.

This recipe originates from the tribe to which I can proudly say I belong – Fante – hence its name Fante-Fante. Once again, this is a well-loved dish yet cooked differently from household to household. Some people steam the fish beforehand, some fry it and some omit the palm oil to make a light soup similar to Nkrakra (Light Soup with Chicken; see page 129). The only universal component is the use of fresh fish – grouper and red snapper are the most popular.

→ **TIPS** Add 1 teaspoon dried ground prawn/shrimp or crayfish powder before steaming for a really pronounced fish flavour.

You can achieve a slightly deeper flavour by sautéeing the onion, chillies and ginger in the palm oil first, then adding the fish and lightly frying for 4–5 minutes. Pour the chalé sauce over the top and simmer for 10 minutes before adding 500ml (18fl oz) water. Bring to the boil, then reduce the heat, cover and simmer for 10–15 minutes until the fish starts to flake, checking intermittently to ensure that the water doesn't completely evaporate and adding more if necessary.

4 medium-large red snapper or halibut fillets (or any white fleshy fish you can muster)

juice of 1 lemon

sea salt

1 onion, diced

3–4 Scotch Bonnet chillies, deseeded and white pith removed if you prefer less heat, diced

7.5cm (3-inch) piece fresh root ginger, grated (unpeeled if organic)

50g (1¾oz) thyme or rosemary (optional)

500ml (18fl oz) uncooked Chalé Sauce (see page 247)

80–100ml (2¾–3½fl oz) sustainable palm oil or carotene oil

coriander, to garnish

Rinse the fish and pat dry with kitchen paper, then squeeze over the lemon juice and sprinkle with sea salt.

Layer the fish pieces into the base of a heavy-based saucepan and pour in just enough water to cover – about 500ml (18fl oz). Add the onion, chillies, ginger, thyme or rosemary (if using) and ½ teaspoon more sea salt, cover and steam over a medium heat for 4–5 minutes.

Add the chalé sauce to the pan and bring to the boil, then reduce the heat and simmer for 4–5 minutes.

Stir in the palm oil gently, trying to avoid breaking up the fish – lightly shaking the pan will prevent the fish sticking to the pan as the juices start to evaporate. Cover and simmer for a further 15 minutes, then check and adjust the seasoning to your taste. Continue cooking, if necessary, until the fish flakes easily.

Serve, garnished with coriander, along with Banku, Savoury Fried Yam or rice with a side of Shito (see pages 169, 33 and 228).

★ Barracuda is quite a full-flavoured fish, so it's not to everyone's taste, but its flesh is really firm and meaty yet super-lean. It can be tricky to get hold of fresh, but can certainly be found frozen in many speciality fishmongers. Like tilapia, it works really well with strong marinades such as Shito made with red chillies or Green Kpakpo Shito Salsa (see pages 228 and 231). Here's an alternative quick and easy way to marinate and cook it.

Fried Barracuda

4 barracuda fillets, defrosted if using frozen

75ml (5 tablespoons) vegetable oil

3–4 eggs

100–150g (3½–5½oz) cornflour

1 teaspoon ground nutmeg

½ teaspoon sea salt

½ teaspoon coarsely ground black pepper

lime wedges, to serve

MARINADE

2.5cm (1-inch) piece fresh root ginger, grated (unpeeled if organic)

1 garlic clove, very finely chopped

1 Scotch Bonnet chilli, deseeded and diced

2 tablespoons crushed or ground grains of paradise (optional)

1 teaspoon sea salt

juice of 2–3 limes

1 tablespoon rapeseed oil or vegetable oil

Mix all the marinade ingredients together in a bowl.

Wash the barracuda fillets in cold water, then drain and pat dry. Add to the marinade and turn to coat thoroughly. Cover the bowl with clingfilm and leave to marinate in the fridge for 1–2 hours.

Heat the oil in a large, deep frying pan over a medium heat. Meanwhile, beat the eggs together in a bowl and mix in the cornflour, nutmeg, sea salt and black pepper.

Dip the fish fillets in the egg and cornflour mixture so that they are evenly coated.

Fry the fillets in the hot oil for 3–4 minutes on each side until evenly golden brown. Remove from the pan and drain on kitchen paper. Serve immediately with lime wedges, Mango and Pineapple Salad, Savoury Fried Yam or Baked Cassava Fries and Simple Fried Plantain (see pages 58, 33, 164 and 42) on the side.

→ **TIP** Barracuda spoils quickly, so keep it well chilled right up to the time of cooking and use within 2 days of purchase.

★ This recipe is a great variation on standard fish cakes – perfect for party food or to serve as a starter. You can use tilapia or haddock instead of red snapper, or any other fish of your choice.

MAKES ABOUT
15 CROQUETTES

Red Snapper & Yam Croquettes

2 tablespoons coconut oil, plus **500ml–1 litre (18fl oz–1¾ pints)** for deep-frying

1 onion, finely diced

2.5cm (1-inch) piece fresh root ginger, grated (unpeeled if organic)

1 garlic clove, very finely chopped or grated

400g (14oz) Oto (Golden Mashed Yam; see page 35)

sea salt, to taste

sugar, to taste

2 teaspoons ground cumin

1–2 teaspoons chilli powder

3 tablespoons chopped coriander

1–2 tablespoons chopped green chillies

2 egg yolks

150–200g (5½–7oz) gari (fermented, dried and ground cassava), or dried white breadcrumbs, for coating

POACHED FISH

500g (1lb 2oz) red snapper fillets, or whole scaled, gutted and washed fish

1 onion, roughly chopped into large chunks

2–3 garlic cloves, crushed

2.5cm (1-inch) piece fresh root ginger, grated (unpeeled if organic)

1 Scotch Bonnet chilli, pierced

6–7 guinea peppers, crushed, or tropical mixed peppercorns

2–3 bay leaves

1 cinnamon stick, or **1 tablespoon** ground cinnamon

1 teaspoon fennel seeds

½ calabash nutmeg, grated, or **1 teaspoon** ground nutmeg

1 star anise (optional)

1 teaspoon sea salt

First poach the fish. Fill a deep saucepan with water, add the fish with the other poaching ingredients and bring to the boil, skimming off the froth that rises to the surface. Reduce the heat and simmer for 12–15 minutes, then remove the fish and set aside to cool. I usually then strain the cooking broth and refrigerate or freeze it for making soup later.

If the fish is on the bone, remove and discard the skin and bones. Place the fish flesh in a bowl and mash with a fork.

Heat the 2 tablespoons of coconut oil in a frying pan, add the onion and cook over a medium heat for a few minutes until translucent. Stir in the ginger and garlic and cook for 3–4 minutes. Stir in the mashed fish and cook for a further 2–3 minutes. Stir in the mashed yam and season to taste with sea salt and sugar. Then add the ground cumin, chilli powder, chopped coriander and green chillies and mix together well.

Leave the fish mixture to cool, then form into about 15 small round patties.

Beat the egg yolks with 2–3 tablespoons water in a bowl. Place the gari or breadcrumbs in a separate shallow bowl or deep plate. Dip each fish patty in turn in the beaten egg, then roll in the gari or breadcrumbs to coat well. (I find it best to double-coat the patties.)

Heat the oil for deep-frying in a deep-fat fryer (the safest option) or heavy-based, deep saucepan filled to just under half the depth of the pan to 180–190°C (350–375°F) or until a cube of bread browns in 30 seconds. Deep-fry the croquettes, in small batches, for a few minutes until browned all over. Remove from the oil and drain on kitchen paper, keeping the cooked croquettes hot while you fry the rest.

Serve with a variety of dips and salsas, such as Avocado & Groundnut Dip, Green Kpakpo Shito Salsa and/or Shito Mayo (see pages 233 and 231).

→ TIP *Turn this into a fish pie by making the fish mixture up to the stage of adding the mashed yam, keeping the poached fish fillets in bigger chunks rather than mashing. Put the fish mixture into an ovenproof dish with 500ml (18fl oz) uncooked Chalé Sauce (see page 247). Top with the mashed yam and grate over a little cheese. Bake in an oven preheated to 160°C (325°F), Gas Mark 3 for about 25 minutes until browned.*

★ While being a very meaty fish, tilapia is also very versatile and when filleted can be quite light. Tilapia can handle a strong marinade but also succumbs very nicely to this more delicate version. If you're used to a bit of punch, why not try making a red or Green Kpakpo Shito Salsa (see page 231) to serve alongside it?

Pan-fried Tilapia Fillets

2 skin-on tilapia fillets

rapeseed oil or coconut oil, for shallow-frying

MARINADE

1 **small** red onion, finely diced

5cm (2-inch) piece fresh root ginger, grated (unpeeled if organic)

2 green kpakpo shito (cherry) chillies, deseeded and finely diced, or substitute green habanero chillies

1 garlic clove, very finely chopped

juice of 1 lime

1 **tablespoon** rapeseed oil or olive oil

2 **tablespoons** ground grains of paradise, or substitute ¼ **teaspoon** ground mace or ½ **teaspoon** ground nutmeg

1 **teaspoon** dried chilli flakes

sea salt and freshly ground black pepper, to taste

Mix all the ingredients for the marinade together in a bowl. Add the tilapia fillets and turn to coat in the marinade, cover the bowl with clingfilm and leave to marinate in the fridge for 1–2 hours.

Remove the tilapia from the fridge a few minutes before you're ready to cook. Heat a little rapeseed oil or coconut oil in a frying pan, add the tilapia fillets, skin-side down, and cook until the edges are crisp. You should find that the fish cooks from underneath in about 8 minutes, as the citrus marinade will have started to gently cook the fish already. You can spoon a little of the hot oil over the top of the fish to finish off the cooking.

Serve on a bed of plain boiled rice with some Green Kpakpo Shito Salsa (see page 231) on top.

★ Deliciously simple and quick, this is a winner at our restaurant and one of my favourite fish dishes. Mackerel is so widely available, it's a sin not to cook it regularly!

In Ghana, smoked mackerel features in many dishes and is sometimes mistakenly called 'salmon' – something to be wary of if actually hoping to buy salmon in a Ghanaian fish market, as it's unlikely to be available!

Simple Grilled Mackerel

4 skin-on mackerel fillets

MARINADE

2 garlic cloves, finely grated

a few sprigs of thyme

2 tablespoons rapeseed oil or olive oil

1 tablespoon lemon juice

½ tablespoon dried chilli flakes

1 teaspoon sea salt

good pinch of coarsely ground black pepper

Mix all the ingredients for the marinade together in a bowl.

Lay the mackerel, skin-side down, on a baking tray lined with greaseproof paper and pour over the marinade so that the fish is evenly coated. Cover with foil and leave to marinate in the fridge for 1–2 hours.

Remove the mackerel from the fridge a few minutes before you're ready to cook and preheat the grill to medium.

Cook the mackerel under the grill for 6–8 minutes, depending on the size of the fish, until just cooked through.

Serve with a side of Crispy Fried Kale, Savoury Fried Yam or Golden Mashed Yam (Oto; see pages 200, 33 and 35) or kenkey (see Tip on page 112).

★ Canned sardines or pilchards in tomato sauce cooked with chalé sauce and served with rice or kenkey was an easy dish that my dad frequently rustled up when we were growing up and was one of the first dishes on my menu when I started putting on supper clubs – just the way Dad used to make it. I still serve this dish today but slightly updated with a couple of twists, using fresh sardines rather than canned and a roasted fresh tomato sauce. It's just as simple and delicious.

Grilled Sardines in a Spiced Roasted Tomato Sauce

½ red onion, sliced

4 **large** ripe tomatoes, quartered

2.5cm (1-inch) piece fresh root ginger, grated (unpeeled if organic)

1 garlic clove, chopped

½ **teaspoon** coarsely ground black pepper

½ **teaspoon** curry powder

½ **teaspoon** extra-hot chilli powder

½ **teaspoon** dried chilli flakes

100ml (3½fl oz) good-quality vegetable or chicken stock

½ **tablespoon** tomato purée

½ **teaspoon** sea salt, plus extra to season

12 whole fresh sardines, scaled, gutted and washed

1 **tablespoon** fresh lemon juice

olive oil, **for drizzling**

ball of Ga kenkey (see Tip, page 112), to serve

Preheat the oven to 180°C (350°F), Gas Mark 4. Line a baking tray with greaseproof paper.

Place all the ingredients except the sardines, lemon juice, oil and kenkey in a bowl and toss together. Spread out on the lined baking tray and roast for 25 minutes.

Remove the tray from the oven and place the sardines on top. Drizzle with the lemon juice and olive oil, and season with an extra pinch of sea salt. Return to the oven and cook for a further 15–20 minutes until the sardines are cooked through.

Meanwhile, prepare the kenkey. Add to a saucepan of boiling water, then reduce the heat slightly and leave to cook for 8–10 minutes or until you can easily insert a fork. Drain and transfer the kenkey to a board or plate. When cool enough to handle, remove the corn cob leaf wrapping, then slice into 8 discs – lots of steam will be released, so be careful.

To serve, lift the cooked sardines gently from the tray to keep them whole for presentation. Place 2 discs of kenkey in the centre of each plate, then ladle over a large spoonful of the roasted tomato sauce and carefully layer 3 sardines on top, making sure they remain intact. Serve with Crispy Fried Kale and a spoonful of Shito (Hot Pepper Sauce; see pages 200 and 228).

★ Think of the perfect warming thick winter soup and mpotompoto (pronounced 'mpo-tom-mpo-toh') ticks all the boxes. This is a famous Ghanaian pottage that has many variations between tribes but is most often prepared with cocoyams (see page 29) and makes a great baby food. I spent much of my weaning years in Ghana and my grandma tells me that I used to gobble this up, making me a very chunky toddler, apparently saying after eating 'pa pa paa' – something like 'best of the best' in the Ghanaian language of Twi. It's super easy to prepare and cooks in no time at all.

Mpotompoto
Cocoyam Pottage

6 cocoyams, peeled and cut into small chunks

1 red onion, finely diced

2.5cm (1-inch) piece fresh root ginger, grated (unpeeled if organic); optional

2–3 tomatoes, diced

1 Scotch Bonnet chilli, pierced (omit if cooking for children or babies!)

about 500ml (18fl oz) good-quality vegetable stock, plus extra if needed

20ml (or 4 teaspoons) sustainable palm oil or carotene oil

120g (4½oz) skinless smoked haddock fillet, or smoked fish of your choice, flaked

½ teaspoon sea salt

½ teaspoon coarsely ground back pepper

1 tablespoon dried ground prawn/shrimp powder

125g (4½oz) crisp fried lardons, for sprinkling (optional)

Peel the cocoyams and cut into 2.5–5cm (1–2-inch) cubes, then rinse thoroughly in cold water to remove the starch.

Add the cocoyam cubes to a saucepan along with the onion, ginger, tomatoes and Scotch Bonnet and pour in enough vegetable stock to cover the ingredients. Bring to the boil and cook for about 10 minutes.

Reduce the heat and leave the pottage to simmer for 20 minutes, while using the back of a wooden spoon to lightly crush the cocoyam pieces – they should already be starting to disintegrate, but this just helps them along.

Carefully fish out the pierced Scotch Bonnet and discard, then, if you have a stick blender, blend the contents of the pot and add a little extra stock if necessary to achieve a soupy consistency.

Add 1 teaspoon of the palm oil along with the flaked smoked fish, sea salt and black pepper, and sprinkle in the prawn/shrimp powder. Stir the pot gently, then leave to simmer for a further 10 minutes or so to ensure that the fish is cooked through and the flavours have combined. Taste and adjust the seasoning if necessary.

Serve in a bowl, drizzled with the remaining palm oil. I like to eat this with crispy lardons sprinkled on top, along with a slice of thickly buttered 'butter bread' or hard dough bread, but good sourdough bread works really well.

→ TIPS You can substitute smoked meats or chorizo for the smoked fish – it's the smoky element that's the important flavour underlying this dish.

If using fish, make sure it's free of all stray bones!

You can also use other types of yam and even sweet potato to make this dish, and/or add other vegetables of your choice, such as carrots and squash.

★ Strolling along the harbour in Jamestown, you see different types and sizes of fish being trawled and hauled, with loud banter and bartering all part of the deal. I didn't expect to see octopus and squid, yet sure enough in lonely, small buckets the apparent runts of the catch sat with no one arguing the toss about them.

Not on the menu of any chop bar or restaurant I visited, and certainly not at Grandma's house, I guess it isn't a common or sought-after seafood. With no traditional recipes to go on, I've devised a few options for Ghana-ifying squid. Each can be shallow- or deep-fried.

SERVES 4 AS A MAIN
SERVES 6 AS A SIDE
OR UP TO 10 AS A PARTY SNACK

Fried Squid

500g (1lb 2oz) cleaned squid
juice of 1 lemon
500ml (18fl oz) water
cayenne pepper, for dusting
shaved fresh papaya, to garnish

BATTER
150-200g (5½-7oz) cornflour
1 teaspoon ground nutmeg
1 teaspoon sea salt
½ teaspoon coarsely ground black pepper
200ml (7fl oz) buttermilk
250-300ml (9-10fl oz) rapeseed oil or vegetable oil

'KEEP IT FRESH' OPTION
50g (1¾oz) shallots or 1 small red onion, finely grated
5cm (2-inch) piece fresh root ginger, grated (unpeeled if organic)
2 garlic cloves, very finely chopped
1 tablespoon crushed grains of paradise (optional)
1 teaspoon cayenne pepper
1-2 teaspoons sea salt, to taste
50-75ml (2-2½fl oz) rapeseed oil or vegetable oil, if shallow-frying

'KEEP IT LIGHT' OPTION
1 heaped teaspoon sea salt
1 teaspoon coarsely ground black pepper
juice of ½ lemon
2 tablespoons Spiced Baobab Butter (see page 232), if shallow-frying

'KEEP IT SPICY' OPTION
2-3 tablespoons Shito made with red chillies (see page 228)
50-75ml (2-2½fl oz) rapeseed oil or vegetable oil, if shallow-frying

Cut the squid into 5mm (¼-inch) rings, as you would calamari. Combine the lemon juice with the water in a small bowl, add the squid and wash gently but thoroughly. Drain and return to the bowl.

★ 'Keep it Fresh'

Using a mortar and pestle, or traditional Ghanaian asanka pot if you have one, grind all the ingredients except the oil together to form a paste, or blitz in a blender. Coat the squid in the paste, then cover and leave to marinate in the fridge for 1 hour.

★ 'Keep it Light'

Season the squid with the sea salt, black pepper and lemon juice and leave to marinate in the fridge for 1 hour.

★ 'Keep it Spicy'

Coat the squid in the shito, and leave to marinate in the fridge for 1 hour.

Remove the marinated squid from the fridge and lightly pat dry with kitchen paper to remove the excess liquid.

If shallow-frying, heat the oil or butter in a frying pan over a medium-high heat. Add the squid and fry for about 6–7 minutes until golden on each side.

To deep-fry the squid, make the batter by beating all the ingredients except the oil together in a bowl and give the marinated squid a generous coating. Heat the oil in a heavy-based, deep saucepan to 180–190°C (350–375°F) or until a cube of bread browns in 30 seconds. Gently drop the squid pieces one by one into the hot oil and fry, in batches, until golden and crispy on all sides. Remove from the oil with a pair of tongs or a slotted ladle and drain on kitchen paper, keeping the cooked squid hot while you fry the rest.

Dust with a pinch of cayenne pepper, garnish with shaved fresh papaya, if you wish, and serve with a variety of dips such as Shito made with red chillies or Jollof Relish (see pages 228 and 234).

→ **TIP** *Soak the squid in the buttermilk for 1–2 hours, before coating in the dry batter mix, to tenderize the squid and increase its sweetness.*

MY GHANA STORY PART 1: GHANA GO HOME

★ I left Ghana as a small child and now I'm returning aged 35. Sitting in the departure lounge at Heathrow Airport's Terminal 5, I think of how it would feel to have someone seeing me off – this is such a big trip! It would feel good. Correction, no – it would be annoying. I like to travel alone. Anticipation rises inside me like a ball atop a fountain. I have been so busy in the weeks and months leading up to this trip that I haven't really had time to be excited, or scared or to think about it all beyond what to pack. I am about to meet most of my dad's family for the first time, embark on a major research trip for my memoir about my relationship with my Ghanaian father and collect as many recipes as I can greedily fit into my journal.

In Kotoka International Airport arrivals lounge, I'm greeted by my Uncle Ernest, who wraps his arms around me warmly, though we are strangers.

'Akwaaba – welcome home – it's been a long time o!'

There is a surprising ease between us, as if we are old friends reunited. It's 6.30am and all of Accra is awake it seems. On our way to Grandma's house in North Kaneshie, I sit in the back of the car incessantly asking questions and snapping through a misty backseat window. Old VW and Mercedes vans repurposed as tro-tros (share taxis) emit a colourful, concatenating sound of low-axle grumbling and men hanging out the side shouting their destinations to pavement passengers – 'Kanesshhhhhh, Kanesshhhhhh, Kanesshhhhhhhh...' The taxis have started their morning bleat for attention, commuting jeeps barge their way through the jams, and motorbikes rip up their own engines making light work of the queues.

Despite the traffic we arrive swiftly at Grandma's small compound. Red dust puffs up to greet us, as do an array of faces to greet me, along with the exclamation, 'I used to change your nappies'. I'm not sure what to reply, so I settle on a laugh.

After a short akwaaba (welcome) ceremony where I am introduced to the family and given water by Grandma, we settle down to the first of three breakfasts. My lifestyle at home means that I'm usually lucky to grab a piece of toast, so this is already an intimidating prospect, and having not yet slept I prepare to be immobilized for the best part of the day.

I've missed the cockerel's full voice, but his presence is apparent. The scratch and swish of Mercy's witch-like broom busily sweeps yesterday's dust out of Grandma's bungalow.

Over a breakfast of rice water, an unflavoured watery bowl of rice with light condensed milk drizzled across it and large hunks of 'butter bread', what I call hard or sweet dough bread, we discuss school systems. Aunty Evelyn is 'taking' waakye for breakfast, I am surprised to see. Rice and beans for breakfast? My internal question is seemingly answered by round two – rice and corned beef stew placed before me, a meal that immediately yet incongruously reminds me of my childhood in London.

We also talk about food. There is an assumption that I don't cook Ghanaian food or eat it very often. They don't yet know that in fact my business at home is running a Ghanaian pop-up restaurant and event catering company. They sit and explain excitedly to me what various local dishes are, such as fufu, kenkey, nkatsenkwan and so on. I politely listen before deciding that I should tell them what I do for a living, since it is part of the reason I am here at all. The strange circularity and serendipity of a recipe hunt, family memoir and reconnection with my roots had forced this trip, one I'd been procrastinating about for most of my life. The visit had finally come to pass because my business and writing demanded it. Who can run a Ghanaian restaurant without ever having been to Ghana? Who can write a memoir about their father when all the answers about him are in Accra?

'Actually, this will make you laugh, but in London I have a small thing where I cook – I mean, I cook Ghanaian food.'

They all stare at me. Aunty Evelyn's eyes bulge open.

'It's called Zoe's Ghana Kitchen, ' I explain optimistically, a little embarrassed.

'Ghana Kitchen,' Francis intones flatly, as if somehow disappointed. He and Evelyn speak in Fante, and I hear the word 'obroni', which is supposed to mean 'foreigner' but in practice means 'white person', used to describe anyone who has light skin from what I can discern; the problems of race are less apparent here. My cousin Geoffrey's head is buried in his large bowl of rice water.

'Yes, it's a pop-up restaurant.'

'Pop-up?'

I go on to explain what this means.

'Ah, so you are a caterer! In Africa we call this a caterer.'

'Yes, sort of, that's right. So it would be great to learn some new recipes while I'm here. To take home, you know?'

'So, you will have to cook for us one day!' Francis declares triumphantly.

I re-adjust my seat. Ghanaian customers always make me nervous, but this is another level. I laugh artificially.

'After you teach me some recipes…'

'No – I want to see what you serve those people in London!'

Everyone, including me, laughs.

★ This is another favourite Fante roadside snack or easy home-cooked meal. The roadside version is usually a little overcooked so that it will keep longer, but this recipe results in a slightly lighter, softer-fleshed version.

Kyenam
Fante Fried Fish with Shaved Papaya

4 whole fresh red snapper, small grouper or trout, scaled, gutted and washed

juice of 2 lemons

sea salt and freshly ground black pepper

50-75ml (2-2½fl oz) rapeseed oil or vegetable oil

MARINADE

5cm (2-inch) piece fresh root ginger, grated (unpeeled if organic)

1 teaspoon ground hot pepper, or substitute cayenne pepper

1 red onion, very finely diced

juice of 1 lemon

1 tablespoon sea salt

1 tablespoon rapeseed oil or vegetable oil (optional)

TO GARNISH

1 red onion, sliced

lemon wedges

1 green or medium-ripe papaya, shaved

Trim the tail of each fish so that they fit neatly into a medium-sized frying pan (a fishmonger will do this for you if you ask nicely). Using a sharp cook's knife, carefully cut 2 evenly spaced diagonal slashes into either side of the fish. Place the prepared fish in a dish.

Using a mortar and pestle, or traditional Ghanaian asanka pot if you have one, grind all the marinade ingredients together to a paste. Alternatively, use a blender, adding the oil if necessary to achieve a paste consistency.

Use half the marinade to rub into the slashes and inside the cavity of each fish, and the other half to coat the fish. Squeeze over the lemon juice and sprinkle sea salt liberally all over, then season with black pepper. Cover the dish with clingfilm and leave the fish to marinate in the fridge for at least 1–2 hours, preferably overnight.

Heat 50ml (2fl oz) oil in a frying pan over a medium-high heat. Once hot, add the fish, in batches and adding the extra oil if necessary, and fry for 4–5 minutes on each side, trying not to move the fish around too much and only turning once, until you've got nice crispy skins.

Remove the fish from the pan and drain on kitchen paper before serving hot with sliced kenkey and Shito (see Tip on page 112 and page 228), garnished with the sliced red onion, lemon wedges and shavings of papaya.

→ **TIP** You can use 150–200ml (5–7fl oz) Shito or Kpapko Shito Salsa, both made with red chillies (see pages 228 and 231) instead for marinating the fish.

★ This dish makes a great, easy starter or snack. I'm not a huge fan of crab meat usually, yet the zesty, peppery combo and bite here with the texture of just-ripe avocado is a winner for me.

Avocado & Crab

1 tablespoon fresh lemon juice

1 garlic clove, very finely chopped

pinch of smoked paprika

¼ teaspoon sea salt

freshly ground black pepper, to taste

1 large ripe avocado

175g (6oz) cooked white crab meat, flaked

TO GARNISH

chopped spring onions

coriander leaves

Mix the lemon juice, garlic, smoked paprika, sea salt and black pepper to taste together in a small bowl.

Using a cook's knife, cut the avocado in half lengthways, then slightly twist the halves to separate them. Holding the avocado half containing the stone firmly and carefully on a chopping board, chop the heel of the knife into the stone and lift it out. Cut through the flesh of each half into cubes, then turn the skin inside out and gently scoop the cubed flesh into the lemon juice mixture in the bowl.

Toss the avocado gently in the lemon mixture – if you mash it, it will go brown and you'll lose that vibrant lush green colour. Mix in the flaked crab meat lightly with a fork.

Serve on toasted sourdough bread or crostini, garnished with chopped spring onions and a sprinkling of coriander.

→ **TIP** *This is also great with crayfish. If using, just sprinkle them on top rather than mixing them in.*

★ Kontomire or Nkontomire is the name given to the leaves of the cocoyam plant in Ghana, also called taro leaves. Taro leaves are quite bitter and the leaves are thicker and tougher than spinach, more akin to kale or spring greens. The simplest substitute for taro is spinach, but you can use whichever greens you prefer.

Kontomire & Apem Stew

cooking salt

400g (14oz) taro or spinach leaves (or spring greens), washed and chopped (see Tips, below right)

6 green kpakpo shito (cherry) chillies or **1–2** Scotch Bonnet chillies, deseeded and diced (adjust the quantity to your taste and desired heat level)

1 teaspoon sea salt

120ml (4fl oz) sustainable palm oil or carotene oil

2 onions, finely diced

3 garlic cloves, very finely chopped (adjust the quantity to your taste)

6–8 ripe tomatoes, preferably plum, diced

¼ teaspoon cayenne pepper

1–2 calabash nutmegs, grated, or substitute **½ teaspoon** ground nutmeg

large pinch of crushed grains of paradise (optional)

4 small whole smoked herring, or fish of your choice (see Tips, below)

2 small whole smoked mackerel, or fish of your choice

1 quantity Apem (see page 41)

100g (3½oz) agushi (dried ground melon seeds)

Put a saucepan of lightly salted water on to the boil to cook the plantains for the apem later. In the process, place the taro or spinach leaves (or spring greens) and chillies in a metal colander or sieve, set over the plantain pan, cover and steam until the leaves have wilted.

Ideally, you would grind the leaves and chillies together with the sea salt in an asanka pot, the traditional Ghanaian mortar and pestle, but otherwise roughly chop or pulse.

Heat the oil in a separate, large saucepan, add the onions, garlic, tomatoes (you can blend these first if you want a very smooth texture), cayenne pepper, nutmeg and grains of paradise, if using, and sauté over a medium heat for a few minutes until the onions are softened.

Meanwhile, break the whole smoked fish into chunky pieces, then gradually add to the pan once the onions are sautéed. Cover and leave to heat through gently for about 20 minutes.

While the stew is cooking, cook the plantains in the pan of boiling water for the apem. Add the taro or spinach leaf mixture to the stew and stir through, then leave over a medium–low heat.

Put the agushi in a bowl and mix in 250ml (9fl oz) water until it resembles scrambled eggs, then add to the stew, stirring it in gently. Serve with the apem.

To eat Ghanaian style, use your hands to scoop up the kontomire with the apem.

➡ TIPS *If using taro leaves or spring greens, remove the tough central stems, then layer up several leaves, roll up together and slice thinly.*

If using dried smoked herring, think ahead and soak them overnight before using. They can be quite chewy otherwise.

Add some al dente steamed or boiled cauliflower to bulk out a vegetarian version of this dish.

Smoked Fish Stew

★ Smoked fish in Ghana is a necessity of the climate – fresh fish doesn't stay fresh for long in the extreme summer heat. It's therefore quite easy to find every kind of fish in smoked form, not just cured as you would expect in the West, for instance in the case of smoked mackerel, but rock-solid preserved! This means it can take a long time to cook through, which is probably why it's so often found in stews and soups where it can sit leisurely unwinding from its smoked coil.

Versions of this dish are to be found across Ghana using locally sourced smoked fish particular to the region. You can pretty much buy any traditional smoked fish from speciality grocers including barracuda, eel, catfish, snapper, grouper and tilapia, but if you can't get your hands on any of these items, good old-fashioned smoked mackerel also works well – as it will already be cooked, just add it along with the carrot at the end.

2 smoked fish of your choice, such as catfish and barracuda

100ml (3½fl oz) sustainable palm oil or groundnut oil

1 onion, diced

1 garlic clove, very finely chopped

5cm (2-inch) piece fresh root ginger, grated (unpeeled if organic)

500ml (18fl oz) uncooked Chalé Sauce (see page 247)

1 Scotch Bonnet chilli, pierced

100ml (3½fl oz) good-quality chicken stock

200g (7oz) peeled yam, cubed and thoroughly washed in cold water

150–175g (5½–6oz) peeled and deseeded butternut squash, cubed (optional)

500ml (18fl oz) water

3–6 whole kpakpo shito (cherry) chillies (optional)

1 large carrot, peeled and sliced

sea salt, to taste

Wash the smoked fish thoroughly and soak in hot water, then cut into medium-sized pieces.

Heat the oil in a large, heavy-based saucepan, add the onion, garlic and ginger and sauté over a medium-high heat, stirring, for 2–3 minutes. Add the smoked fish and stir well to coat in the oil and seasonings before mixing in the chalé sauce. Add the pierced Scotch Bonnet, cover and bring to the boil, then reduce the heat and leave to simmer over a medium heat. After 10 minutes, pour in the stock and continue to simmer for a further 5–10 minutes.

Add the yam, butternut squash, if using, the measured water, and the kpakpo shito chillies, if using, then simmer for 20–25 minutes, or until the vegetables are tender.

Stir in the carrot and simmer for a further 10 minutes.

Season to taste with salt before serving with rice (cooked as you like), Fufu (see page 173) or boiled yam.

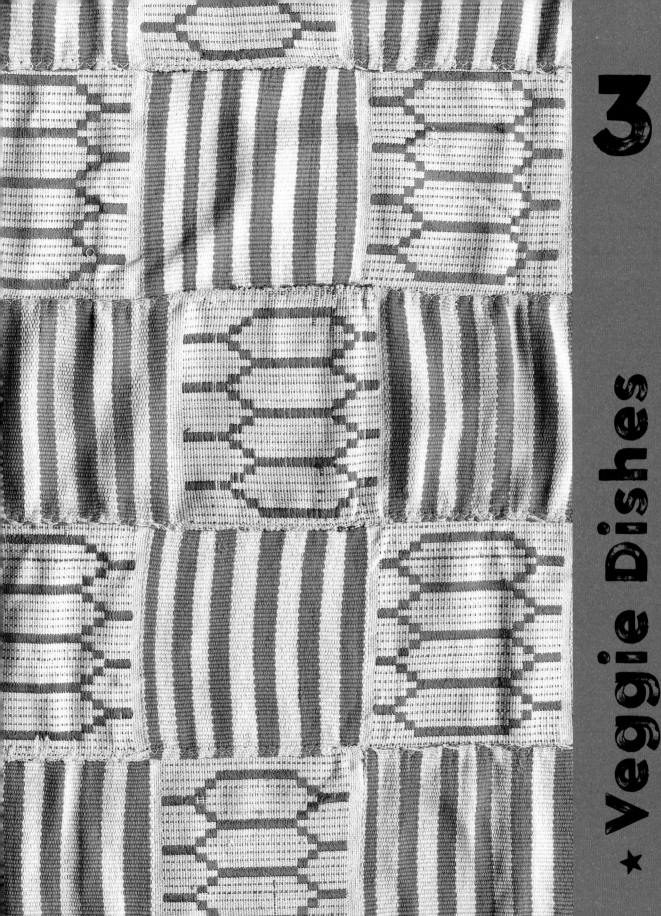

3

★ Veggie Dishes ★

★ Here's my twist on traditional Kontomire or nkontomire stew (*see* page 95) – a delicious vegan spinach curry, to which you can add extra steamed veg of your choice to make it into a more substantial meal.

Spinach & Agushi Curry

1 tablespoon coconut oil

1 small onion, thinly sliced

2 teaspoons curry powder

1 teaspoon chilli powder

350ml (12fl oz) uncooked Chalé sauce (see page 247)

100g (3½oz) or about **2 heaped tablespoons** agushi (dried ground melon seeds)

8 guinea peppers, crushed (optional)

juice of 1 lime

150-300ml (5-10fl oz) water or good-quality vegetable stock, if required

200g (7oz) baby leaf spinach

1 teaspoon sea salt

1 teaspoon coarsely ground black pepper

GRILLED PLANTAIN (OPTIONAL)

4-6 ripe plantains

1 tablespoon ground ginger

½ tablespoon dried chilli flakes

sea salt

coconut oil (melted) and olive oil, **for drizzling**

Heat a large, heavy-based saucepan and add the coconut oil. When it has melted, add the onion and sauté over a medium heat for a few minutes until softened, then add the curry and chilli powders and stir well. Stir in the chalé sauce and simmer over a low heat for 20 minutes.

Gently stir in the agushi, using the back of a wooden spoon to break down any lumps that may form – the sauce should start to turn creamy and resemble scrambled eggs. Add the guinea peppers, if using, and the lime juice. Leave to simmer over a medium heat for a further 10 minutes. If the sauce becomes too thick, add the water or vegetable stock a little at a time to loosen it. The colour of the stew will have changed from pink to a mustard colour.

Stir in the spinach and sea salt and black pepper, then simmer gently until the spinach has wilted.

Meanwhile, prepare the grilled plantain, if making. Preheat the grill to medium-high. Using a sharp knife, peel the plantains by cutting the tips off each end and slicing through the skin lengthways (avoid cutting into the flesh), then use your hands to remove the skin. Cut the plantains in half lengthways. Rub with the ground ginger, chilli flakes and sea salt, and drizzle with coconut or olive oil. Grill for 12–15 minutes, turning over halfway through. Serve alongside the spinach curry.

★ While *santom/abrodwomaa* is generally the Ghanaian name for sweet potatoes, a pretty common sight in markets and kitchens, in the northern region of Ghana the orange-fleshed variety most of us are familiar with has been christened *alafie wuljo* in the local language of Dagbani, meaning 'healthy potato'. This is because it has been introduced relatively recently through a USAID project to counter vitamin A deficiency, and has proven a big hit. Here's just one of many ways to spin a roasted sweet potato.

Roasted & Stuffed Spiced Sweet Potato

4 sweet potatoes, scrubbed

olive oil, **for drizzling**

3 red peppers

1 red onion, diced

1 red Scotch Bonnet chilli, deseeded and diced

1 **bunch** of spinach, shredded

3 garlic cloves, crushed

1 **teaspoon** Ghanaian Five-spice Mix (see page 244)

sea salt

½ **bunch** of coriander, chopped

4 **tablespoons** crème fraîche (optional)

freshly ground black pepper

Preheat the oven to 200°C (400°F), Gas Mark 6.

Start by placing the sweet potatoes on a baking tray and drizzle lightly with olive oil, zigzagging it across the potatoes. Bake for 20–25 minutes until they are soft in the middle.

Place the red peppers on a separate baking tray, drizzle lightly with olive oil and bake alongside the potatoes for about 20 minutes until soft.

While the potatoes and peppers are baking, coat the base of a saucepan with olive oil, add the onion and sauté over a medium heat for a few minutes until transparent.

Stir in the chilli, spinach and garlic, season with the five-spice mix and ½ teaspoon sea salt and cook until the spinach has slightly softened.

Remove the roasted red peppers and sweet potatoes from the oven. Shred the peppers, discarding the cores and seeds, and add to the spinach mixture, then stir in most of the chopped coriander.

Using a sharp knife, make an incision down the middle of each sweet potato (without going all the way through or touching either end), then push it gently so that the hole opens up. Take a large spoonful of the spinach mixture and gently push into the hole, but you want some of the mixture to remain on the outside. Place a tablespoonful of crème fraîche (if using) on top with a little chopped coriander. Season to taste with sea salt and black pepper and serve on a small bed of rocket on a plate.

→ **TIP** Use a fork to pierce the roasted sweet potatoes to test that they're light and fluffy inside.

Aboboi

Bambara Bean Stew

★ This wonderful creamy bean stew is a summer favourite most often served with Tatale (see page 43). It is beloved in Ghana and one of our chefs in Brixton – a fellow Fante, 'Aunty' Cynthia – takes particular pride in cooking this dish. Cynthia always insists on soaking the beans overnight as we do in the restaurant, but at home I find that, as with black-eyed beans, you can save time by just boiling them in salted water.

300g (10½oz) dried bambara beans, or substitute dried chickpeas

1½ red onions, finely chopped

½ teaspoon sea salt, plus extra to taste

200g Romano peppers, cored, deseeded and roughly chopped

3–4 red rocket (Anaheim) chillies, roughly chopped

10g (¼oz) thyme leaves, roughly chopped

olive oil, for drizzling

7.5cm (3-inch) piece fresh root ginger, grated (unpeeled if organic)

2 garlic cloves, very finely chopped

½ tablespoon ground hot pepper, or substitute cayenne pepper, or 1 small red bird's-eye chilli, deseeded and diced

1 tablespoon granulated or soft light brown sugar

3 tablespoons dried ground prawn/shrimp powder (optional – omit for a veggie version)

Preheat the oven to 180°C (350°F), Gas Mark 4, and line a baking tray with greaseproof paper.

Place the beans in a heavy-based saucepan and cover with water (about 750ml/1¼ pints). Add half the chopped onions and the salt and bring to the boil, then continue to boil, stirring regularly, for 2–3 minutes, skimming off any froth that rises to the surface. Reduce the heat and simmer, uncovered, for 1–2 hours or until the beans are just tender. Add a little extra water as required to the pan to prevent it running dry.

While the beans are simmering, spread the peppers, chillies and thyme out on the lined baking tray, drizzle with olive oil and roast for 25 minutes.

Transfer the roasted peppers and chillies to a blender or food processor, add the remaining onions and the ginger, garlic and ground hot pepper and blitz until well blended. Pass the mixture through a sieve to remove any remaining bits, then add to the pan of beans along with the sugar and ground prawn/shrimp powder (if using).

When most of the liquid in the pan has evaporated, you should be left with a rich, creamy bean stew. Adjust the seasoning to your taste at the end, then serve in a bowl with a light sprinkling of gari (fermented, dried and ground cassava) and a side of Tatale (see page 43).

→ **TIP** *The cooking times of dried beans can vary depending on how long they've been dried for so one batch can take 2 hours and another 3–4 hours — be prepared to wait if you're not pre-soaking them overnight.*

★ Quite simply this is a Ghana-fied version of chana dhal!

Ghana Dhal

250g (9oz) yellow dried split peas, thoroughly washed in cold water until it runs clear

1 green Scotch Bonnet chilli, pierced

3 tablespoons coconut oil

1 tablespoon cumin seeds

1 small onion, diced

3–4 whole green kpakpo shito (cherry) chillies, pierced

5cm (2-inch) piece fresh root ginger, grated (unpeeled if organic)

250ml (9fl oz) uncooked Chalé Sauce (see page 247)

1½ teaspoons ground coriander

¾ teaspoon ground turmeric

¾ teaspoon Ghanaian Five-spice Mix (see page 244)

½ teaspoon ground hot pepper, or substitute cayenne pepper

sea salt and freshly ground black pepper

handful of chopped coriander

Place the split peas in a heavy-based saucepan and cover with water (about 850ml/1½ pints). Add the pierced Scotch Bonnet, stir through and bring to the boil, skimming off the froth that rises to the surface.

Cover the pan, reduce the heat and simmer, stirring regularly, for 35–40 minutes or until the split peas are just tender, adding more water as necessary.

Remove the pan from the heat, fish out the Scotch Bonnet and use a stick blender or whisk to break the split peas down. Leave to cool.

Heat 1 tablespoon of the oil in a separate saucepan, add the cumin seeds and cook over a medium heat for 30 seconds or so until fragrant. Add the onion, chillies and ginger and sauté for 4–5 minutes or until the onion is golden.

Add the remaining 2 tablespoons oil to the pan along with the ground spices and 2 tablespoons water and stir well, then add the chalé sauce and stir thoroughly so the mixture is well blended.

Simmer over a medium heat for 15 minutes – the oil should start to rise to the surface, at which point you can stir the cooked split peas into the sauce. Bring the mixture to the boil for a few minutes, adding more water as necessary to loosen it, then season to taste with sea salt and black pepper.

Stir in the chopped coriander just before serving, or use as a garnish, and serve with toasted hard dough bread, Coconut Rice (see page 172) or grilled plantain.

★ This recipe makes a lovely vegetable curry.

Cocoyam & Sweet Potato Curry

1-2 sweet potatoes, peeled and diced

rapeseed oil, for **drizzling and frying**

sea salt and freshly ground black pepper

2 bay leaves, torn

2-3 cocoyams, peeled and diced

1 red onion, sliced

2 garlic cloves, crushed

5cm (2-inch) piece fresh root ginger, grated (unpeeled if organic)

2 teaspoons cornflour

1 teaspoon cayenne pepper

1 teaspoon curry powder

1 teaspoon ground coriander

1 teaspoon ground turmeric

½ teaspoon ground nutmeg

½ teaspoon ground cinnamon

3 green chillies, such as bird's-eye, chopped

200ml (7fl oz) coconut milk, or almond milk

250-300ml (9-10fl oz) good-quality vegetable stock

Preheat the oven to 220°C (425°F), Gas Mark 7.

Spread the diced sweet potatoes out on a baking tray, drizzle with a little oil, season with sea salt and black pepper and scatter with the torn bay leaves. Roast for 15–20 minutes until soft and slightly crisp at the edges.

In a pan of lightly salted boiling water, par-boil the diced cocoyam for 8-10 minutes. Drain and set aside

Meanwhile, heat a little more oil in a large, heavy-based saucepan, add the onion and sauté gently for a few minutes until it turns golden. Add the garlic and ginger and cook for a further 2 minutes. Sift in the cornflour, then add the spices and chillies and stir well.

Pour in the milk and bring to a simmer, stirring continuously to avoid lumps forming. Continue to simmer, stirring frequently, for 5–10 minutes.

Add the drained par-boiled cocoyam and then gradually stir in the vegetable stock until you have the consistency you want. Simmer for a further 25–30 minutes or until the cocoyam is really tender, stirring regularly to make sure it doesn't stick to the pan.

Finally, stir in the roasted sweet potato and serve with plain boiled rice.

Nkruma Nkwan
Okra Soup & Banku

★ This is one of my favourite dishes to encourage people to change their minds about okra, lest they might otherwise miss out on its incredibly rich flavour. A famous West African dish, it traditionally calls for you to finely chop the okra and then boil it separately, the purpose and result of which is to create a very slimy okra sauce. I'm not a fan of slimy okra, so instead I slice mine slightly less than 1cm (½ inch) thick rather than dicing it. The smaller you cut the okra, the more it will release the mucilage inside the pods, a process only further developed by boiling, so by adding the sliced okra straight to the stew, you can be sure to avoid slimy okra soup.

You can also vary or bulk out this dish by adding fried fish (croaker or catfish and tilapia work really well), goat meat (kid goat on the bone will infuse it with great flavour), beef or chicken. But it's just as tasty as a purely vegetarian dish.

→ **TIP** *Shop-bought banku is just as good as making your own — most African grocers will have one of those red- or blue-coloured cool boxes with a stock of ready-made fresh or vacuum-packed Ga kenkey or banku hiding inside. It's very affordable and comes in packs of two, which is more than enough for this recipe. Just boil it for 8—10 minutes so that it is malleable, as it's supposed to be eaten with your hands. However, if you feel like taking up the challenge, a recipe for homemade Banku is on page 169.*

200ml (7fl oz) sustainable palm oil or carotene oil

2 red onions, finely diced

2 garlic cloves, very finely chopped or grated

7.5cm (3-inch) piece fresh root ginger, finely grated (unpeeled if organic)

1 Scotch Bonnet chilli, deseeded and diced

500g (1lb 2oz) ripe plum tomatoes, diced

1 tablespoon tomato purée

250ml (9fl oz) good-quality vegetable stock

500g (1lb 2 oz) okra, trimmed and sliced

150ml (5fl oz) water

sea salt and freshly ground black pepper, to taste

shop-bought banku, to serve (see Tip, below left)

Heat the oil over a medium–low heat until it melts (palm oil has a low smoke point, so be careful not to let it burn), add the onions and sauté gently for a few minutes until translucent. Add the garlic, ginger and Scotch Bonnet and stir well, then sauté for a further 5 minutes.

Add the tomatoes and tomato purée to the pan and stir well, then pour in the vegetable stock, reduce the heat to low, cover and simmer for 15 minutes.

Add the okra to the pot with the measured water, replace the lid and simmer for a further 20 minutes until the okra is just tender. Season to taste with sea salt and black pepper.

This dish is traditionally served in a bowl with banku on a side plate (see Tip, left) – a few slices is all you'll need, as it's very dense – along with a finger bowl.

Gari Foto
Savoury Gari with Eggs

★ Gari – fermented, dried and ground cassava – is a strange ingredient because it has no real flavour of its own apart from the sourness of fermentation. However, it's one of those staples that can take on a great deal of flavour and bulk out meagre pickings in the fridge.

As a child I used to sneak a bowl of gari porridge with hot water and a pinch of salt with a good dollop of Dad's shito (hot pepper sauce) on the side as a snack before dinner when I got home from school, and could demolish the bowl in a few minutes, 'hiding' the evidence in the sink, soaking.

→ **TIP** *Just recently I tried cracking a couple of eggs into the centre of the pan after folding the gari into the stew, then putting the pan under the grill, shakshuka style, for a few minutes, and it was super-tasty and a nice twist on the dish.*

120ml (4fl oz) sustainable palm oil or groundnut oil

2 onions, finely diced

1cm (½-inch) piece fresh root ginger, grated (unpeeled if organic), or ½ teaspoon ground ginger

1 garlic clove, very finely chopped, or ¼ teaspoon garlic powder

2 fresh red chillies, deseeded and finely chopped, or ¼ teaspoon ground hot pepper, or substitute cayenne pepper

3 large ripe tomatoes, roughly chopped

1 scant tablespoon tomato purée

250g (9oz) gari (fermented, dried and ground cassava)

120ml (4fl oz) lightly salted warm water

6 eggs

sea salt and freshly ground black pepper

chopped coriander, to garnish (optional)

Heat the oil in a frying pan, add the onions and sauté over a medium heat for about 3 minutes until translucent.

Add the ginger, garlic and chillies and stir well to evenly coat the onions before adding the chopped tomatoes and tomato purée. Leave to cook over the medium heat for about 25 minutes.

As soon as you've added the tomatoes, start preparing the gari, which is a little like preparing couscous. Place it in a bowl and gradually sprinkle with the measured lightly salted warm water to evenly moisten it, mixing it through with a fork as you go – be careful to add the water a little at a time so that you don't overdo it, as the mixture should just be damp, not drenched!

Cover the bowl with a plate or clean cloth and set aside for 10–15 minutes while you prepare the eggs.

At this point, choose how you want to cook your eggs and prepare them. If it's the weekend and I fancy a treat, I might poach the eggs, but if I feel like something more everyday, I might just boil or scramble them. It's up to you.

Before adding your choice of cooked eggs to the dish, fold the moistened gari into the stew, which should be cooked by now, and stir through gently but thoroughly – you should get a nice pink colour to the mixture. If you've prepared scrambled eggs, you can also fold them into the gari now to create a sort of gari omelette, or serve them on the side.

Remove the pan from the heat and season to taste with sea salt and black pepper. Serve immediately, with the seasoned poached, boiled or scrambled eggs on top, if that's what you've opted for, garnished with some chopped coriander if you have it.

Red Red Stew

★ This dish is so called, I'm told, because it's coloured red twice – once from the red of the palm oil and a second time from the tomatoes. But there's a lot of duplication in the titles of dishes in Ghanaian cooking in any case. This stew of black-eyed beans (cowpeas) cooked in a gently spiced tomato sauce is a great vegan dish eaten all day long in Ghana – an alternative to baked beans for breakfast or as a bean casserole for lunch or dinner. Usually eaten with Simple Fried Plantain (see page 42), this is tasty, nourishing comfort food that's super-easy to make.

200g (7oz) dried black-eyed beans, or 400g (14oz) can organic black-eyed beans

75ml (5 tablespoons) sustainable palm oil or carotene oil

1 red onion, finely diced

2.5cm (1-inch) piece fresh root ginger, finely grated (unpeeled if organic)

½ tablespoon dried chilli flakes

½ red Scotch Bonnet chilli, deseeded and diced

½ teaspoon curry powder

½ tablespoon chilli powder

400g (14oz) can chopped or whole plum tomatoes

200g (7oz) plum tomatoes, roughly chopped

1 tablespoon tomato purée

1 teaspoon sea salt

½ teaspoon freshly ground black pepper

gari (fermented, dried and ground cassava), for sprinkling

If using dried beans, rinse and place in a large saucepan, cover with a good depth of water and bring to the boil, then simmer for at least 1 hour or until the beans are tender enough to be squeezed easily between thumb and forefinger. Drain and set aside. If using a can of beans, just drain, rinse and drain again.

Heat the oil in a large, heavy-based saucepan over a low–medium heat until it melts (palm oil has a low smoke point, so be careful not to let it burn), add the onion, ginger, chilli flakes and Scotch Bonnet and sauté gently for a few minutes until the onion is translucent. Add the curry and chilli powders and stir well.

Add all the tomatoes, tomato purée, sea salt and black pepper and stir through. Leave to cook over a medium heat for 45–60 minutes or until the tomatoes start to break down. If you want a smooth sauce, blend with a stick blender at this point.

Add the cooked or drained canned beans, reduce the heat to medium–low and cook for a further 30 minutes, stirring occasionally so that the beans don't stick to the pan, until the beans are tender and the tartness of tomatoes has dissipated.

Check the seasoning before serving in a bowl with some gari sprinkled on top, along with a side of Simple Fried Plantain (see page 42).

→ **TIP** *If using canned chopped tomatoes, add them 20 minutes into the cooking time or stir in 1 tablespoon sugar to counterbalance the tartness of the tomatoes.*

MY GHANA STORY PART 2:
My Big Fat Ghanaian Breakfast(s)

★ Breakfast has been happening around three times a day. Well, for me anyway. Ghanaian hospitality is such that my Grandma insists on feeding me as many times as possible. I stay in bed each morning, the fan above spinning sympathetic, slightly-cooled air down at me as I lie scared and motionless. To make a sound, a creak – even to blink too loudly – would within minutes mean a plate of food presented to me before my morning wee.

MY AVERAGE BREAKFASTING ROUTINE AT GRANDMA'S:

6.15am – Wake up.

6.30am – Mercy prepares a flask of hot water so I can 'take' tea and butter bread. Here, 'tea' means any hot drink – I have a choice of Milo, Ovaltine, sachet instant coffee or, more recently, Lipton's English Breakfast tea (I am being spoilt). I love butter bread and Ovaltine, so this is in no way fair.

7.00am – Omelette and 'beef' sausages.

7.30am – Rice water or oats.

9.00am – Yams or rice with chicken, goat or mixed meat stew.

9.30am – Go back to bed for a nap to steel myself for lunch.

I'm pretty sure – in fact I know – that no one else in the house is eating such frequent and lavish breakfasts. They have huddled together and unanimously decided to fatten up the skinny *obroni* – ehh ehh.

On Palace Street, there is, according to my Uncle Francis, the best waakye in Accra. At 6am every morning, before his 'home breakfast', he joins a queue across the road (funny how convenience improves on flavour) and waits to fill a polythene bag with waakye stew of mixed meats in spiced tomatoes, with rice and beans, noodles, a boiled egg and shito (Ghana's

traditional hot pepper sauce made with smoked ground prawns). On the opposite corner, you can find the city's best kelewele (diced and fried plantain in fresh ginger and grated onion), which he may run to for an afternoon snack.

Francis will then disappear for an hour – probably for a nap.

While Francis is out exploring his neighbourhood's finest street food offerings, I am chained to the hospitality chair being forcibly fed what my generous hosts think equates to an English breakfast.

Street food is embedded in everyday life here. Morning, noon and night, grills on street corners boast the heady scent of things charring. Street hawkers' chop bars and street food vendors are the fabric of the dietary day in Kaneshie.

Pedestrians pound into work every day amid a swirling commotion, often stopping for breakfast at a street food cart. I've never been so excited to watch a commute as I was there; the rattling city waking up for work has a kind of cinematic cacophony of traffic, bustle and grill smoke.

Aunty Evelyn 'takes' either waakye for breakfast or rice water. Rice water is as it sounds – boiled rice and water – you can add sugar or evaporated milk, it's pretty much the same as Ambrosia creamed rice, just less sweet and more tasty.

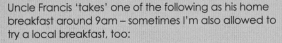

Uncle Francis 'takes' one of the following as his home breakfast around 9am – sometimes I'm also allowed to try a local breakfast, too:

Mpotompoto – Cocoyams chopped into little pieces and boiled, then you add a little salt and pepper and palm oil.

Tom Brown – Fried then grounded maize (corn) mixed with water and made into porridge, taken with butter bread (the sweetest I've tasted, with hints of cinnamon and aromas reminiscent of hot cross buns).

Kokoo – Ground maize (not fried) also mixed with water. This has the consistency of baby food or a certain brand of chicken soup from a can. It tastes like smelted kenkey – that's because they are different forms of the same thing: ground maize. As with kenkey, it's pretty bland so I added sugar and carnation milk. It was still pretty bland. Not wanting to offend, I ate the whole never-ending bowl, but suggested it could do with spicing up, to which Francis replied "Oh yes… Hausa Kokoo – this one has spices and such blended in – I think you will like this one." So my mission is to track down some Hausa Kokoo before I leave and will definitely experiment with it when I get home.

Uncle Francis loves kokoo and ate a bucket bowl of it. He recommends it for 'when you are ill or have a fever and can't take food – it makes you wee a lot and the fever disappears,' he explains with a hearty laugh.

★ This is another simple way to re-spin my favourite basic peanut sauce, this time teaming it with some juicy lamb cutlets or chops. Simply reheat the sauce if you've pre-made it, or have some left over from another recipe, and spoon over the lamb when it's cooked.

Lamb Cutlets with Peanut Sauce

8 lamb cutlets or chops, about 2cm (¾ inch) thick

1 quantity Peanut Sauce (see page 249)

MARINADE

3 tablespoons rapeseed oil or groundnut oil

2.5cm (1-inch) piece fresh root ginger, finely grated (unpeeled if organic)

1 tablespoon cayenne pepper

1 teaspoon sea salt

1 teaspoon coarsely ground black pepper

TO GARNISH

a few roughly chopped roasted peanuts

sprinkle of finely sliced spring onion

Place the lamb cutlets or chops in a dish. Mix all the marinade ingredients together in a bowl, pour over the lamb and rub the mixture thoroughly into the meat, coating it all over. If you have time, cover the dish with clingfilm and leave to marinate in the fridge for 1 hour.

Meanwhile, prepare the peanut sauce, or reheat it if you have pre-made a batch.

Take the lamb out of the fridge and leave it to return to room temperature for a few minutes while you heat a griddle pan over a high heat until very hot. Add the lamb cutlets or chops – they should sizzle on contact – and then reduce the heat slightly. Cook the meat without disturbing it (see Tip below), allowing it to sear evenly and obtain even griddle marks, then flip and repeat. (If you move the meat around during the cooking process, it will be likely to stick to the pan and won't cook evenly.)

Remove the lamb from the pan and leave to rest for 1 minute before transferring to warmed serving plates. Pour 1–2 tablespoons of the peanut sauce over each of the cutlets or chops, then add a little garnish of chopped roasted peanuts and finely sliced spring onion. Serve with rice and Simple Fried Plantain (see page 42), with a green salad on the side.

→ **TIP** Cooking times for the lamb cutlets will vary depending on their thickness. As a guide, cook for 2–3 minutes if you want your meat pink or 4–5 minutes if you prefer it well-done.

Kyinkyinga
Suya Goat Kebabs

★ Suya is the term used in Ghana to refer both to a groundnut spice rub, also called *tankora*, and a popular West African style of street-food cooking – grilled skewered meat, also known as *kyinkyinga*. Basically, it's the Ghanaian answer to the shish kebab.

You can choose whatever meat you fancy for this recipe. (*See* also Suya Beef Kebabs overleaf). I've used kid goat because its gamey tenderness is perfect with suya and goat is the most common version I've come across in Accra, but also because my Uncle Ernest loves it. Cook it on the barbecue during the summer, or enjoy it all year round cooked in a griddle pan or under the grill. Whichever, it's super-simple and tasty as hell.

1 quantity Suya Spice Rub (see page 246)

2 tablespoons rapeseed oil

450g (1lb) boneless leg of kid goat, diced

1–2 peppers, cored, deseeded and cut into chunks (the colour is up to you, but I like to use a combo of red, yellow and green: Ghana's national colours)

1 large red onion, quartered

1 tablespoon groundnut oil, or vegetable oil

1 teaspoon sea salt

1 teaspoon coarsely ground black pepper

TO GARNISH

2–3 tablespoons coarsely chopped roasted peanuts

small pinch of ground hot pepper, or substitute cayenne pepper or chilli powder

a few coriander leaves

If using bamboo skewers, presoak in water for about 1 hour to prevent them burning.

Mix the spice rub with the rapeseed oil in a bowl. Add the goat to the bowl and massage the mixture thoroughly into the meat.

Thread the chunks of pepper, onion and goat on to your skewers – I use 10–13cm (4–5-inch) bamboo skewers, which will fit on at least 3 cubes of meat with the other ingredients.

As ever, the longer you can leave the ingredients to marinate the better, so if you have time, lay the skewers in a dish, cover with clingfilm and leave in the fridge for at least 1–2 hours, but preferably overnight if you're organized and have planned ahead.

Take the skewers out of the fridge and leave them to sit at room temperature for a few minutes while you prepare a charcoal barbecue or preheat a gas barbecue, griddle pan or grill to medium-high heat.

Brush the meat with the groundnut oil and season with the sea salt and black pepper before adding to the barbecue or griddle pan or putting under the grill. The kebabs should sizzle as they hit the grill or griddle, but don't move them too quickly. Turn them at 2 minute intervals until each side is seared for medium-rare, or give them 3 minutes each side for well done.

Remove from the heat and leave to rest for 2 minutes.

Serve with a side of fresh seasonal salad leaves, garnished with the coarsely chopped peanuts, ground hot pepper or chilli powder and coriander leaves. Boom! An explosion of summer spice in your mouth!

★ Another great summer dish paying homage to Kyinkyinga (see previous page) and the ever-versatile suya spice rub. Be warned, the spice level here packs a punch.

Suya Beef Kebabs

40–50g (1½–1¾oz) Suya Spice Rub (see page 246)

1kg (2lb 4oz) lean beef rump tail, trimmed and cubed

1 red onion, quartered, then separated into layers

1 green and 1 red or yellow pepper, cored, deseeded and cut into chunks

groundnut oil, for brushing

sea salt and freshly ground black pepper

ADDITIONAL FRESH SEASONINGS

1 tablespoon groundnut oil

5cm (2-inch) piece fresh root ginger, grated (unpeeled if organic)

1 garlic clove, very finely chopped

TO GARNISH

pinch of ground hot pepper, or substitute cayenne pepper

pinch of freshly ground roasted peanuts

pinch of finely chopped green bird's-eye chilli

sprinkling of chopped coriander

Place 2 tablespoons of the Suya Spice Rub in a large bowl, add the additional fresh seasonings and mix together. Add the beef and work the mixture into all sides of the meat. Cover the bowl with clingfilm and leave to marinate in the fridge for at least 1 hour, preferably overnight. If using bamboo skewers, presoak in water for about 1 hour to prevent them burning.

Remove the beef from the fridge and thread on to skewers, alternating with the onion and pepper chunks – 3 pieces of beef per skewer. Brush with groundnut oil and season with sea salt and black pepper.

Heat a griddle pan over a high heat until very hot. Add 3 kebabs – they should sizzle on contact – and cook without disturbing for 1 minute, pressing the meat on to the surface of the pan using a pair of tongs. Then turn and repeat until each side is seared. Remove the kebabs from pan and leave for the oil to drain off and the meat to rest for 1 minute. The total cooking time should be 5 minutes – the juices should run clear but the meat will still be slightly pink inside and juicy, rather than dry and overcooked.

Sprinkle the kebabs with ground hot pepper, ground peanuts, chilli and coriander and serve with Scotch Bonnet Coleslaw, Jollof Relish or Garden Egg Dip (see pages 64, 234 and 170).

★ Here's another way to re-style a dinner menu standard – marinate some lean red meat in a suya spice rub, slice and cook up some yam and you've got yourself steak and chips Ghanaian style!

Suya Steak Bavette

2 bavette steaks, about **250g (9oz)** each

25–30g/1oz Suya Spice Rub (see page 246)

1 teaspoon groundnut oil

ADDITIONAL FRESH SEASONINGS

2 tablespoons groundnut oil
(sunflower oil will do)

5cm (2-inch) piece fresh root ginger,
grated (unpeeled if organic)

3 garlic cloves, very finely chopped
or grated

sprig of thyme, leaves picked

TO GARNISH

1 teaspoon roughly chopped
roasted peanuts

1 teaspoon finely chopped green
bird's-eye chilli

1 teaspoon chopped coriander

pinch of ground hot pepper, or substitute
cayenne pepper

To tenderize the steak, gently pound with the back of a wooden spoon on both sides on a chopping board. Place in a dish.

Mix the Suya Spice Rub with the additional fresh seasonings in a bowl. Add the mixture to the steak dish and rub into the tenderized meat evenly. Cover the dish with clingfilm and leave to marinate in the fridge for at least 1 hour, preferably overnight.

Take the meat out of the fridge and leave it to return to room temperature for a few minutes while you heat a griddle pan over a high heat until very hot and brush with the groundnut oil. Add the steak – it should sizzle on contact – and cook without disturbing it for 2 minutes, allowing it to sear evenly and obtain even griddle marks, then flip and repeat. (If you move the meat around during the cooking process, it will be likely to stick to the pan and won't cook evenly.) If necessary, continue cooking the meat until done to your liking.

Remove the steak from the pan and leave to rest for 2–3 minutes before serving, garnished with the chopped peanuts, chilli, coriander and ground hot pepper. Serve with a small ramekin of Peanut Sauce (see page 249), some Chunky Yam Chips (see page 36) and a green salad.

★ This light and spicy broth is so wholesome and warming. It's my go-to dish on chilly winter days to stave off cold symptoms...and works every time!

Nkrakra
Light Soup with Chicken

2kg (4lb 8oz) or 8-10 bone-in, skinless chicken thighs

1 onion, finely diced

handful of thyme sprigs

4-5 guinea peppers, cracked open

1 **teaspoon** extra-hot chilli powder

3 garlic cloves, finely diced

2 **teaspoons** sea salt

500ml (18fl oz) uncooked Chalé Sauce (see page 247)

1 **litre (1¾ pints)** hot good-quality chicken stock

freshly ground black pepper

400g (14oz) mixed peeled (where appropriate) and diced vegetables, such as yams or sweet potatoes, carrots and white cabbage (optional)

sprig of coriander, to garnish (optional)

Place the chicken in a large, heavy-based saucepan or flameproof casserole dish with the onion, thyme, guinea peppers, chilli powder, garlic and 1 teaspoon of the sea salt. Cook together over a low heat, partially covered, until the juices start to run from the chicken.

Pour the chalé sauce over the chicken mixture, then cover and simmer for about 30 minutes until the chicken juices run clear.

Stir in the hot stock and bring to the boil, then reduce the heat and simmer for about 1 hour until the chicken is tender. Season to taste with black pepper.

Add your choice of vegetables, if desired, and cook until tender. You can remove the sprigs of thyme before serving.

I love to serve this dish in a traditional Ghanaian asanka pot with a ball of Fufu on the side (see page 173), as it looks so inviting that way. You can also serve it on its own in a large bowl garnished with a sprig of coriander, or with a slice of slightly toasted sourdough bread on the side.

→ **TIP** If you're happy to go low and slow while cooking, this dish is perfect for cheaper cuts of chicken such as from older hens or broiling hens — you get tons of extra flavour but need to slow cook for 3-4 hours over a low heat.

★ This mildly spiced, hearty beef stew is the definition of comfort food. Once it's all in the pot, you can get some other bits and bobs done while it's cooking away, but whomever you're feeding will think you've been slaving away all day!

Kontomire Froe
Beef & Spinach Stew

rapeseed oil or vegetable oil, for browning and sautéeing

1kg (2lb 4oz) rump tail, cubed

1 onion, finely chopped

2 garlic cloves, finely chopped

500ml (18fl oz) uncooked Chalé Sauce (see page 247)

5cm (2-inch) piece fresh root ginger, finely grated (unpeeled if organic)

4 serrano chillies, diced (deseed to reduce the heat level)

1 Scotch Bonnet chilli, pierced (optional)

2 green peppers, cored, deseeded and thinly sliced

250ml (9fl oz) good-quality beef stock

1 teaspoon sea salt

freshly ground black pepper

250g (9oz) baby leaf or sliced spinach

Heat 1 tablespoon of oil in a large, heavy-based saucepan over a medium-high heat, add the beef in batches and cook until browned all over, adding another 1 tablespoon of oil to the pan to brown each batch. Remove from the pan and set aside in a bowl.

Heat another 1 tablespoon oil in the same pan, add the onion and garlic and sauté over a medium heat until the onion softens and begins to turn golden.

Add the chalé sauce and cook, stirring, to avoid it sticking to the pan. Stirring in some of the accumulated juices from the beef will also help to prevent the mixture from sticking to the base of the pan and burning.

Add the ginger, serrano chillies, Scotch Bonnet (if using) and green peppers and cook, stirring, for several minutes.

Stir in the beef stock, then return the beef and its accumulated juices to the pan and season with the sea salt and black pepper.

Reduce the heat to low, cover and simmer for 1–2 hours or until the beef is almost falling apart.

Stir in the spinach and cook for about 5 minutes until it has wilted.

Serve the stew in a bowl with a side of plain boiled white rice or Golden Mashed Yam (Oto; see page 35).

★ This is a winner for any party or barbecue. Who doesn't love ribs? This sticky plantain sauce lifts them to a whole new level!

Pork Ribs in Sticky Plantain Sauce

1.5kg (3lb 5oz) rack pork spare rib

500ml (18fl oz) good-quality vegetable stock

2 bay leaves, torn

2 red onions, sliced

2 garlic cloves, crushed

½ bunch of thyme

6 guinea peppers, cracked open, or tropical mixed peppercorns

STICKY PLANTAIN SAUCE

25ml (1fl oz) olive oil

2 red onions, sliced

2 garlic cloves, very finely chopped

1 tablespoon Ghanaian Five-spice Mix (see page 244)

1 Scotch Bonnet chilli, diced

½ teaspoon dried chilli flakes

75-80g (2½-2¾oz) soft dark brown sugar

2 tablespoons tomato purée

50ml (2fl oz) port

2-3 teaspoons cornflour, mixed with cold water to a smooth paste

1 large ripe plantain, peeled and cut into chunks

sea salt and coarsely ground black pepper

Place the rib rack in a large, deep heavy-based saucepan, pour over the stock to cover and add the bay leaves, onions, garlic, thyme and guinea peppers or peppercorns. Bring to the boil, then reduce the heat, cover and simmer for 1 hour, or until the meat is tender.

While the ribs are simmering, make the sticky plantain sauce. Heat a frying pan until hot, add the olive oil, onions and garlic and sauté over a medium heat for a few minutes until the onions have softened. Add the five-spice mix, Scotch Bonnet, chilli flakes and sugar and cook for 1–2 minutes until the sugar has dissolved.

Stir in the tomato purée, port and about 50ml (2fl oz) stock from the ribs. Add the cornflour paste and plantain and bring to the boil, stirring, then reduce the heat and simmer for 15 minutes until thickened. Season to taste with sea salt and black pepper. Meanwhile, preheat the oven to 180°C (350°F), Gas Mark 4.

Remove the sauce from the heat and leave to cool slightly, then transfer to a blender or food processor and blend to a smooth paste.

Remove the rack of ribs from the pan and place on a baking tray. Spoon the sauce over the ribs, turning to make sure they are completely coated, and roast for 30–40 minutes or until sticky and heated through.

Remove the baking tray from the oven and slice the rack into individual ribs. Place on a sharing board or individual plates and serve with a side of Scotch Bonnet Coleslaw (see page 64).

★ Fetri detsi (pronounced 'fedree-ditchi') is a variation on the Okra Soup theme (see page 112) – a Ewe version with many of the same ingredients but with a different infusion of flavours. This recipe was given to me when I spent some time up in the Volta region in Ho, as a guest of the charity/non-governmental organization KickStart Ghana, where I was introduced to some local Ewe takes on what I knew to be Fante dishes. Feel free to go light on the okra if you're not a fan.

Antoinette's Ewe Fetri Detsi

4 bone-in chicken portions (optional)

100g (3½oz) trimmed okra, sliced

1–2 bunches of spinach or greens of your choice, roughly chopped

1 tablespoon dried ground prawn/shrimp powder

150–200g (5½–7oz) mixed smoked herring and mackerel fillets (optional)

1 large onion, diced

2 garlic cloves, very finely chopped

5–7.5cm (2–3-inch) piece fresh root ginger, grated (unpeeled if organic)

75g (2¾oz) green kpakpo shito (cherry) chillies

1 tablespoon ground hot pepper, or substitute cayenne pepper

1 teaspoon sea salt

250ml (9fl oz) uncooked Chalé Sauce (see page 247)

250ml (9fl oz) sustainable palm oil or carotene oil

If using chicken (you can serve it just with the smoked fish), fry, roast or grill your chicken as you like it.

Meanwhile, add the okra to a large, heavy-based saucepan of boiling water so that it's just covered, along with the spinach or other greens and stir in the prawn/shrimp powder, then add the smoked herring and mackerel (if using).

Using a mortar and pestle, or a traditional Ghanaian asanka pot if you have one, blend the onion, garlic, ginger, kpakpo shito chillies, hot pepper or cayenne and salt together to make a loose pulp and add to the pan, then stir in the chalé sauce and palm oil. Cover the pan and leave to cook over a low heat for about 1 hour, adding the chicken (if using) once it's cooked, or until the palm oil rises to the surface.

Fish out (excuse the pun!) the herring and mackerel (if used) and keep for another day, or serve instead of or as well as the chicken.

Voila! That's tasty – thanks Antoinette!

→ **TIP** You can turn this into a vegan dish by simply omitting the fish and chicken, or vary it by using salted instead of smoked fish, such as mackerel.

★ This is another variation on the Spinach & Agushi stew (see page 102), known endearingly as palaver sauce. As with many Ghanaian dishes, arguments rage about how it should be made. Bone-in lamb works so well with this dish, it's simply got to be tried. You can also make a veggie or a fish version.

Lamb Palaver

500g (1lb 2oz) bone-in leg of lamb, cubed

2 garlic cloves, crushed and very finely chopped

4cm (1½-inch) piece fresh root ginger, grated (unpeeled if organic)

1 Scotch Bonnet chilli, pierced

a few sprigs of thyme

4 guinea peppers, cracked open

1 teaspoon curry powder

1 tablespoon freshly ground coriander or ½ **tablespoon** coriander seeds

½ teaspoon ground nutmeg

½ teaspoon ground cinnamon

½ teaspoon chilli powder

1 red onion, sliced

500ml (18fl oz) uncooked Chalé Sauce (see page 247)

200g (7oz) agushi (dried ground melon seeds)

150g (5½oz) baby leaf or chopped spinach

Place the lamb with the garlic, ginger, chilli, herbs, spices and onion in a large, heavy-based saucepan over a medium heat. Cover and leave to steam in its own juices for 20–25 minutes until the lamb juices run clear.

Add enough water to just cover the meat and to create a stock. Bring to the boil, skimming off any froth that rises to the surface, then reduce the heat and simmer for at least 45 minutes until the meat is tender and the stock reduced.

Stir in the chalé sauce and continue to simmer over a low heat for 25 minutes.

Sprinkle in the agushi a little at a time, stirring well, until the sauce starts to resemble over-scrambled eggs.

Just before serving, stir in the spinach until it has wilted, then serve with Waakye Rice (see page 162), plain steamed rice or Golden Mashed Yam (Oto; see page 35).

⟶ **TIP** You can use boneless lamb here instead but the bones provide extra flavour.

★ Good Ghanaian food doesn't get much simpler than 'stew', and every household is reared on the stuff. In the West, tenderness is usually valued in cooked meat, but in West Africa chewy, slightly overcooked meat is the norm, and that is true of this dish also. If you want to attain a softer bite here, you can reduce the cooking time by about 10 minutes.

Simple Beef Stew

500g (1lb 2oz) lean chuck steak, cubed

8 guinea peppers, cracked open

1 tablespoon black peppercorns

1 red onion, quartered

1-2 sticks celery, chopped

1 sprig of thyme

1 teaspoon sea salt, or to taste

3 tablespoons vegetable oil

1 large white onion, diced

1 teaspoon curry powder

½ teaspoon chilli powder

500ml (18fl oz) uncooked Chalé Sauce (see page 247)

1 teaspoon ground white pepper

1 teaspoon cayenne pepper

TO GARNISH

chopped parsley

chopped basil

finely chopped coriander

finely sliced green bird's-eye chilli

Place the beef, guinea peppers, black peppercorns, onion, celery and sea salt in a large, heavy-based saucepan, pour in enough water to just cover the beef and bring to the boil. Reduce the heat and simmer for 30–40 minutes until the beef is tender. Strain and reserve the stock.

Add 1 tablespoon of the oil to the same pan, add half the beef and cook until browned all over. Remove from the pan and set aside. Repeat with the remaining beef, adding another 1 tablespoon of oil if needed.

Heat the remaining 1 tablespoon oil in the same pan, add the white onion and sauté over a medium heat for a few minutes until translucent. Add the curry powder and chilli powder and stir well.

Pour in the chalé sauce, add the white pepper and cayenne pepper and bring to the boil. Reduce the heat and simmer for about 30 minutes, stirring regularly and adding the reserved beef stock as needed to prevent the sauce sticking to the pan.

Adjust the seasoning if necessary, then serve garnished with chopped parsley, basil or coriander and finely sliced bird's-eye chilli.

★ By far the most popular dish on both our street-food and restaurant menus is this super-crispy and succulent fried chicken recipe – I really shouldn't be giving away the secret!

SERVES 4

Jollof Fried Chicken

2 tablespoons Jollof Dry Spice Mix (see page 244)

½ teaspoon sea salt

½ teaspoon coarsely ground black pepper

1 tablespoon rapeseed oil

4 boneless, skinless chicken breasts, cut into strips

250ml (9fl oz) buttermilk

500ml–1 litre (18fl oz–1¾ pints) vegetable oil, for deep-frying

COATING

150–200g (5½–7oz) cornflour

½ teaspoon coarsely ground black pepper

½ teaspoon sea salt

1 teaspoon ground nutmeg

Mix the jollof dry spice mix, sea salt and black pepper with the rapeseed oil in a large bowl. Add the chicken strips and buttermilk and turn to coat them all over. Cover the bowl with clingfilm and leave to marinate in the fridge for at least 1–2 hours, preferably overnight.

Heat the oil in a deep-fat fryer (the safest option) or heavy-based, deep saucepan filled to just under half the depth of the pan to 180–190°C (350–375°F) or until a cube of bread browns in 30 seconds.

Meanwhile, put the cornflour in a separate bowl with the seasoning and nutmeg and mix well.

Dip each chicken strip into the seasoned cornflour to coat evenly – try to do 4 or 5 pieces in quick succession, as you need to drop them into the hot oil straight away.

Fry the chicken, in batches, for no more than 3–4 minutes to keep them succulent and juicy yet cooked through, and golden and crispy but not burnt. Remove from the oil and drain on kitchen paper, keeping the cooked chicken hot while you fry the rest.

It's that easy – the best fried chicken you're ever going to eat! Serve with Jollof (One-pot Rice), Scotch Bonnet Coleslaw or Chunky Yam Chips, with a side of Shito Mayo (see pages 142, 64, 36 and 231).

★ The inspiration for this recipe came from Josie, the Law School Secretary while I was at the University of Greenwich. Josie shared with me the secret of her Italian family's slow-cooked steak ragu with mashed broccoli and garlic, and I've never cooked ragu with minced meat since! The addition of guinea peppers to the stew gives it a certain lift and a Ghanaian twist. This is a low and slow cook, but it's worth the wait and a perfect winter warmer.

Goat Ragu

1 **tablespoon** sunflower or rapeseed oil

2 onions, diced

3 **garlic cloves**, very finely chopped or grated

3 **bay leaves**

1 **tablespoon** chopped rosemary

1 **tablespoon** dried chilli flakes

1 **teaspoon** ground nutmeg

1 **teaspoon** dried oregano or dried mixed herbs

1 **teaspoon** sugar

450g (1lb) boneless leg of kid goat, cubed

good pinch of sea salt and 1 **teaspoon** coarsely ground black pepper, or more to taste

150ml (5fl oz) red wine

2 **tablespoons** tomato purée

10 **large** plum tomatoes, diced, or 400g (14oz) can plum tomatoes

175ml (6fl oz) good-quality beef stock, or about 100ml (3½fl oz) if using fresh tomatoes

2 carrots, peeled (if not organic) and grated

sprig of basil, to garnish

MASHED BROCCOLI

2 **heads** of broccoli, cut into chunks (including stems)

cooking salt

25g (1oz) Spiced Baobab Butter (see page 232)

2 **garlic cloves**, very finely chopped

Heat the oil in a large, heavy-based saucepan over a medium-low heat, add the onions and gently sauté for 6–7 minutes until soft and translucent.

Stir in the garlic, bay leaves, rosemary, chilli flakes, nutmeg, oregano or mixed herbs and sugar and sauté for a further 3 minutes.

Increase the heat to medium-high, add the kid goat and leave to brown for a few minutes, then season with the sea salt and black pepper.

Pour in the red wine and stir to deglaze the pan, scraping up all the residue from the base, then add the tomato purée and tomatoes and top up with the beef stock. Bring to the boil, then reduce the heat, cover and simmer for 2½ hours.

About 20 minutes before the end of the cooking time, stir in the grated carrots and check the seasoning, adding extra sea salt and black pepper if required.

At this point, add the broccoli to a saucepan of salted boiling water and cook for 4–5 minutes until fork tender. Drain and mash loosely with a fork together with the butter and garlic.

To serve, transfer the ragu to a large sharing bowl for people to help themselves and garnish with the basil. Serve with some warmed sliced baguette and the mashed broccoli. Delicious!

Jollof
One-pot Rice

★ Jollof is a one-pot rice dish akin in essence to Jambalaya or even Paella (depending on the ingredients you use). It is by far and away West Africa's most readily available and consumed dish, also known as 'party rice' because of its frequent centre-stage role at dinner party tables and banquets. Believed to originate from the Senegalese dish *benachin* in the Wolof language or 'one-pot rice', there are many arguments between Nigerians and Ghanaians about who makes the best jollof and variations exist in Sierra Leone, Togo, Liberia and beyond. In Cameroon they use coconut milk and in Gambia they bake it.

Almost everyone familiar with jollof has their own recipe for it, and nobody else's version is as good as their mother's or grandma's, but the principle is always rice cooked in a spiced blend of tomatoes and onion, which gives it its rich red colouring. What epitomizes Ghanaian jollof for me is the sweet, smoky heat from Scotch Bonnet chilli (giving just enough robust heat to warm the palate without having to reach for a glass of soothing milk) and the distinctive smoky fish flavour from the dried ground crayfish or prawn/shrimp powder. I've used chicken here but you can use whatever meat and vegetables take your fancy (*see* Tips, right).

2 large onions, finely chopped

olive oil or groundnut oil

6–8 bone-in chicken portions (thighs or drumsticks)

2 garlic cloves, very finely chopped

1 tablespoon thyme leaves

1 large bay leaf

5–6 guinea peppers, crushed

1 Scotch Bonnet chilli, deseeded and diced

2 tablespoons Jollof Dry Spice Mix (*see* page 244)

1 teaspoon sea salt

4 tablespoons groundnut oil or sunflower oil

1 teaspoon hot chilli powder

1 teaspoon curry powder

500ml (18fl oz) Jollof Sauce (*see* page 248)

300g (10½oz) basmati or other long-grain white rice

chopped parsley or coriander, to garnish

Shito (Hot Pepper Sauce) or Green Kpakpo Shito Salsa (*see* pages 228 and 231), to serve

★ Stage 1

First make the broth. Sweat half the chopped onion in a little oil in a large, heavy-based saucepan over a low heat, add the chicken, the garlic, thyme, bay leaf, guinea peppers, Scotch Bonnet, 1 tablespoon jollof dry spice mix and sea salt and stir well. Pour in enough water just to cover the ingredients and bring to the boil, then reduce the heat and simmer for 20 minutes or until the chicken is tender.

Meanwhile, preheat the oven to 180°C (350°F), Gas Mark 4.

Remove the chicken from the pan, place on a baking tray and drizzle with olive oil or groundnut oil. Bake in the oven for 20–25 minutes.

Drain the fragrant broth into a jug and reserve for adding to the rice.

★ Stage 2

To make the jollof, heat the 4 tablespoons of groundnut or sunflower oil in the same pan you used to make the broth, add the remaining chopped onion and sauté over a medium heat for a few minutes until soft. Stir in the remaining jollof dry spice mix, the chilli powder and curry powder and add 350ml (12fl oz) of the jollof sauce, reserving the rest for adding at the next stage. Then stir the broth into the pan.

★ Stage 3

Wash the rice thoroughly in cold water to remove as much starch as possible – I wash it in at least 3 changes of water until the water runs clear – then drain and stir it into the jollof sauce/broth mixture so that it's evenly coated. Ladle in the reserved jollof sauce without stirring, then reduce the heat, cover the pan with foil to keep in the steam and add the lid. Cook for 15–20 minutes until all the liquid has been absorbed and the rice is tender. Stir through with a fork to fluff up the rice.

By this stage, your chicken in the oven should be perfectly crisp! Serve the rice with the chicken pieces on top, scattered with the chopped herbs to garnish, with shito or kpakpo shito salsa on the side.

→ **TIPS** If the sauce isn't hot enough before adding the rice, the rice will soak up the cold water and become soggy.

If you find that the rice is too dry halfway through cooking, top up with additional water, adding a small quantity at a time as needed.

You can make this an even meatier dish by adding lamb, beef or goat, but you can also turn it into a delicious vegetarian dish by adding garden eggs (African aubergines), carrots and peas or other mixed vegetables and excluding the ground crayfish or prawn/shrimp powder from the jollof dry spice mix, or try the recipe for Veggie Jollof on page 146.

★ It's fascinating to note how the basic principles of certain dishes cross over from one national cuisine to another. When describing jollof to someone who has never tried it before, I use paella or jambalaya as examples of comparable one-pot rice meals. It's another of Ghana's flexible dishes that can be just as easily prepared with seafood or as a vegetarian option, as in the version below, in which you can use any vegetables you like.

Veggie Jollof

1 **tablespoon** groundnut oil or vegetable oil

1 **onion**, diced

1 **teaspoon** curry powder

1 **teaspoon** chilli powder

2 **tablespoons** Jollof Dry Spice Mix (see page 244)

500ml (18fl oz) uncooked Chalé Sauce (see page 247)

300–350g (10½–12oz) basmati or other long-grain white rice, thoroughly washed in cold water until it runs clear, then drained

150g (5½oz) peas

3 carrots, peeled (if not organic) and sliced or diced

Green Kpakpo Shito Salsa (see page 231), to serve

Heat the oil in a large, heavy-based saucepan, add the onion and sauté over a medium heat until golden. Add the curry powder and chilli powder and stir through gently, then stir in the jollof dry spice mix.

Add the chalé sauce to the pan and stir well, then continue to cook, covered, over a medium heat for 20–25 minutes.

Stir in the rice and bring the mixture to the boil. Add the peas and carrots and stir through, then reduce the heat, cover the pan with foil to keep in the steam and add the lid. Cook for 20 minutes until all the liquid has been absorbed and the rice is tender. Stir through with a fork to fluff up the rice, then serve with kpakpo shito salsa on the side.

★ It's not uncommon in Ghana for meat and fish to be cooked together in one-pot dishes, and this dish is Ghanaian surf and turf at its best. You can change up the meat or fish to whatever suits your palate.

Ntroba Froe
Garden Egg & Okra Stew

450g (1lb) bone-in lamb shoulder or beef, cubed

1 large onion, diced

2 large garlic cloves, very finely chopped

5cm (2-inch) piece fresh root ginger, grated (unpeeled if organic)

1 Scotch Bonnet chilli, pierced

2 guinea peppers, cracked open (optional)

about 500ml (18fl oz) good-quality vegetable stock

1 aubergine, cut into 2cm (¾-inch) cubes

8 garden eggs (African aubergines), trimmed and cut into 2cm (¾-inch) cubes

olive oil, for drizzling

sea salt

2–3 tablespoons sustainable palm oil or carotene oil

8 okra, trimmed and thinly sliced

750ml (1⅓ pints) uncooked Chalé Sauce (see page 247)

1–2 tablespoons dried ground prawn/shrimp powder, or **1 tablespoon** Shito (Hot Pepper Sauce; see page 228)

200g (7oz) skinless smoked fish fillets, such as smoked haddock or smoked mackerel, flaked (see Tips, below)

4 uncooked soft-shell crabs or prawns

Put the meat in a large, heavy-based saucepan with the onion, garlic, ginger, Scotch Bonnet and guinea peppers (if using) over a medium heat. Cover and leave to steam for 20–25 minutes until the meat juices run clear.

Add enough vegetable stock to cover the meat, reduce the heat and simmer for a further 25–30 minutes, skimming off any froth that rises to the surface, until tender – the meat should fall away easily from the bone when tested with a fork.

While the meat is stewing, preheat the oven to 200°C (400°F), Gas Mark 6. Spread the garden egg cubes out on a baking tray, drizzle with a little olive oil and season with sea salt, then roast for 20 minutes.

Heat the palm oil in a frying pan, add the okra and fry for a few minutes over a high heat until crisp, then set aside.

Transfer half the roasted garden egg to a blender, add a little water and blend to a purée.

Add the chalé sauce to the meat pot and stir through, then add the puréed garden egg along with the prawn/shrimp powder (or shito), fish and seafood and cook for 15 minutes over a medium heat.

Add the remaining roasted garden egg and the crispy okra, along with its cooking oil, and simmer for a further 5 minutes.

Serve hot with freshly boiled yam and Simple Fried Plantain (see page 42).

→ TIPS *Instead of roasting, you can steam or boil the garden egg, which will give the dish a looser, softer texture.*

If using smoked haddock or other raw fish, rub it with a little Ghanaian Five-spice Mix (see page 244), pan-roast it in a bit of oil until cooked and add to the pot before serving, or serve the stew over the pan-roasted fish.

Corned Beef Stew

★ This recipe brings back so many memories of childhood, mostly of the uncommon silence between my sister and me while we were chomping our way through it. It's such simple and economical fare and yet so good for the soul! Don't be put off by the idea of using canned corned beef – it's a dish that has surprised a lot of people previously unacquainted with such pleasures. You can of course buy corned beef from the butcher, but the canned variety is just so handy. Mum also loved this one because it was dinner done and dusted in 20 minutes flat.

2 **tablespoons** rapeseed oil or sunflower oil

1 onion, diced

1 **teaspoon** extra-hot chill powder

1 **teaspoon** curry powder

750ml (1⅓ **pints**) uncooked Chalé Sauce (see page 247)

350g (12oz) canned corned beef

2 carrots, peeled (if not organic) and diced

75g (2¾oz) peas

4 soft-boiled eggs

Heat the oil in a large, heavy-based saucepan, add the onion and sauté over a medium heat along with the chilli powder and curry powder for a few minutes. Stir in the chalé sauce.

Divide the corned beef into 4 equal pieces (which avoids arguments over portions later!), or break it up into the sauce, then add the carrots and peas. Leave to simmer for 15–20 minutes. You may find that the sauce starts to dry out, so add a little water if necessary.

Peel the boiled eggs and slice in half, then add them to the stew. Cook for a further 5 minutes.

Serve with boiled yams and plantain or rice – either way, it will vanish in no time!

Nkatsenkwan
Peanut Butter/Groundnut Stew with Lamb

★ Nkatsenkwan, as this dish is known in Ghana, is most frequently eaten with Fufu (pounded green plantain or yam with cassava – see page 173), but you can also serve it with boiled yams, cassava or even rice. It's equally good served on its own as a rich winter stew with a sprinkling of gari (fermented, dried and ground cassava) and a side of fried sweet plantain (see Simple Fried Plantain, page 42).

This recipe is for lamb (or mutton), but it can be made with any combination of meat and seafood. There is a traditional Fante version of the recipe on my blog that features large forest snails and crabs for the adventurous palate!

2kg (4lb 8oz) mixed bone-in lamb (or mutton) neck and shoulder, cubed

500ml (18fl oz) water or good-quality vegetable stock

1 onion, finely diced

5cm (2-inch) piece fresh root ginger, grated (unpeeled if organic)

1 garlic clove, crushed

8 green kpakpo shito (cherry) chillies, or substitute 1–2 Scotch Bonnet chillies, pierced, according to desired level of heat

1 tablespoon extra-hot chilli powder

1 tablespoon curry powder

2 teaspoons sea salt

1 teaspoon freshly ground black pepper

500ml (18fl oz) uncooked Chalé Sauce (see page 247)

100–200g (3½–7oz) organic peanut butter, depending on how thick you want it

1 red Scotch Bonnet chilli, pierced

3 tablespoons crushed roasted peanuts, to garnish

Put the lamb into a large, heavy-based saucepan, cover with the measured water or stock and add the onion, ginger, garlic, kpakpo shito chillies, chilli powder, curry powder, sea salt and black pepper. Bring to the boil, then reduce the heat and simmer over a medium heat for 25 minutes until the lamb juices run clear, skimming off any froth that rises to the surface.

Stir in the chalé sauce and then add the peanut butter 1 tablespoon at a time while stirring until it has all dissolved. Add the pierced Scotch Bonnet and cook for a further 45 minutes–1 hour over a low heat, stirring regularly so that the sauce doesn't stick to the pan, until the peanut oil has separated and risen to the top, which means that it's done. You should have a soupy consistency and super-tender meat falling away from the bone.

Serve with your choice of side dish (see the recipe introduction), or with crushed roasted peanuts or gari sprinkled on top.

→ TIP To speed up this recipe, steam the lamb with the onion and ginger until the meat juices run clear, pour over 600ml (20fl oz) Peanut Sauce (see page 249), add the pierced Scotch Bonnet and simmer for 45 minutes–1 hour, or until the meat is falling away from the bone.

★ These make a great starter or finger food for parties, and are really simple and fast to make.

Jollof Spiced Chicken Skewers

750g (1lb 10oz) chicken breast strips

2 tablespoons rapeseed oil

2 tablespoons Jollof Dry Spice Mix (see page 244)

pinch of sea salt

1 teaspoon freshly ground black pepper

TO GARNISH

chopped coriander

strips of spring onion

Preheat the grill to medium. Line a baking tray with foil.

Mix all the ingredients together in a bowl, making sure that the chicken pieces are evenly coated in the oil, spices and seasoning.

Thread the chicken on to skewers (if using bamboo skewers, presoak in water for about 1 hour to prevent them burning), then space them out on the lined baking tray. Alternatively, simply skip the skewering and lay the chicken pieces out separately on the lined tray so that they cook evenly.

Cook under the grill for 20–25 minutes, turning halfway through the cooking time – the aim is to ensure succulent, tender chicken, so don't let it overcook!

Serve garnished with chopped coriander and strips of onion along with Jollof Relish, Shito (Hot Pepper Sauce) or Shito Mayo (see pages 234, 228 and 231) for dipping and a side salad.

→ **TIP** You can add this cooked chicken to a batch of reheated Jollof Relish (see page 234) to make a great chicken stew that can be served with Jollof (One-pot Rice; see page 142) or plain boiled rice.

★ The palm tree is the wonder tree; there isn't a part of it – from its leaves to its roots – that goes unused. The leaves are used for constructing shelters or making brooms for sweeping, the fruits (nuts) for soup, palm oil and vegetable oil, and the trunk is tapped for the highly intoxicating, naturally-fermented palm wine, while the rest is burned as fire wood. The colourful red fruits are to be seen overflowing from baskets in markets, which are then pounded with a large mortar and pestle and the pith removed to leave their distinctive rich red, nutty oil.

This dish is another one-pot wonder that can be combined with any meat, fish, poultry or shellfish of your choice.

Abenkwan
Palm Soup

500g (1lb 2oz) rump or chuck steak, cubed

200g (7oz) smoked fish fillets or cooked crab meat

1 whole dried salted tilapia (preferably pre-soaked overnight) chopped into 4 pieces

2 onions, chopped

2 garlic cloves, crushed (optional)

4 teaspoons tomato purée

½ teaspoon sea salt

2 red rocket (Anaheim) chillies, deseeded and white pith removed if you prefer less heat, diced, or substitute 1 tablespoon dried chilli flakes

1 green habanero or Scotch Bonnet chilli, pierced, or 4-5 whole green kpakpo shito (cherry) chillies

1 tablespoon extra-hot chilli powder

1 teaspoon dried thyme or 20-25g (¾-1oz) fresh thyme leaves

5-8cm (2-3-inch) piece fresh root ginger, grated (unpeeled if organic)

3 dried bay leaves

350-400ml (12-14fl oz) sustainable palm oil or carotene oil, or 600g (1lb 5oz) canned palm nut paste mixed with 1-2 litres (1¾-3½ pints) water

200g (7oz) tomatoes, diced

100g (3½oz) okra, trimmed

1 aubergine, cut into chunks (optional)

Put the beef in a large, heavy-based saucepan with the fish or crab meat, dried tilapia, onions, garlic (if using), tomato purée and sea salt over a medium heat, stir well, cover and leave to steam in its own juices for about 10 minutes.

Stir in the chillies (or chilli flakes), chilli powder, thyme, ginger and bay leaves, then replace the lid and simmer for about 10 minutes.

Mix in the palm oil, or palm nut paste and water, and cook for 15 minutes over a medium heat.

Add the tomatoes, okra and aubergine, if using, and bring to the boil. Reduce the heat and simmer for at least 1 hour, uncovered, until the soup has thickened, stirring occasionally to prevent the soup from burning.

Serve with Fufu, kenkey (see page 173 and Tip on page 112) or boiled yams or rice.

★ Suya is a mixture of ground peanuts and spices used to coat meat before cooking. It's very quick and simple to prepare, yet adds a unique taste and texture. A Ghanaian twist on a well-known and loved dish, these meatballs make a great dinner, or summer barbecue party fodder Ghanaian street-food style, inspired by Kyinkyinga (see page 124).

Suya Spiced Lamb Meatballs or Koftas

450g (1lb) minced lamb

1 onion, finely chopped

2 garlic cloves, crushed

2.5cm (1-inch) piece fresh root ginger, grated (unpeeled if organic)

2 green bird's-eye chillies, finely chopped

4 tablespoons natural yogurt

3 tablespoons Suya Spice Rub
(see page 246)

1 egg yolk, beaten with
2 tablespoons water

Light a charcoal barbecue or preheat a gas barbecue to medium-high heat, or preheat the oven to 200°C (400°F), Gas Mark 6.

Mix the lamb, onion, garlic, ginger, chillies, yogurt and 1 tablespoon of the dry spice mix together in a large bowl.

Place the beaten egg yolk mixture in a bowl and the remaining 2 tablespoons dry spice mix in a separate shallow bowl or deep plate. Form the lamb mixture into about 12 evenly sized balls, or sausage shapes for koftas. Dip each meatball or kofta in the beaten egg yolk mixture and then roll in the spice mix until evenly coated.

Cook on the barbecue for 6–8 minutes, turning regularly, or on a baking tray in the oven for 10–15 minutes until cooked through. Serve with Jollof Relish and Peanut Sauce (see pages 234 and 249) for dipping and a big Ghana Salad or Jollof (One-pot Rice; see pages 52 and 142).

★ This is one of Ghana's most loved dishes. As with many traditional recipes, a number of variations exist. The stew often comes with an assortment of meats and fried fish, but you can make it without and it's still waakye stew. For intensity and richness of taste I suggest using goat meat or mutton, but it's patience that delivers the full flavour here – this dish is at its best when cooked slowly with love and, if possible, allowed to sit overnight, since as with many stews it tastes even better the next day.

SERVES 4-6

Waakye Stew

450-500g (1lb-1lb 2oz) boneless leg of goat or mutton, cubed

1 garlic clove, very finely chopped, or ½ teaspoon garlic powder

1 teaspoon soft light brown sugar (granulated will do if you don't have any)

½ tablespoon sea salt, plus extra to taste if needed

1 teaspoon smoked paprika

½ teaspoon ground turmeric

1 teaspoon cornflour

150ml (5fl oz) groundnut oil

3 large red onions, finely diced

1 teaspoon ground hot pepper, or substitute cayenne pepper

10g (¼oz) crushed guinea pepper or grains of paradise.

5cm (2-inch) piece fresh root ginger, grated (unpeeled if organic)

10 red rocket (Anaheim) chillies, or 2 red Scotch Bonnet chillies, deseeded, if you want it really hot

125g (4½oz) tomato purée mixed with 150ml (5fl oz) water to a smooth paste

10-12 or 650g (1lb 7oz) plum or any good-quality ripe tomatoes, cut into chunks

3 large red Romano or regular peppers, cored, deseeded and cut into chunks (optional)

1 teaspoon Ghanaian Five-spice Mix (see page 244)

1 tablespoon dried ground crayfish or prawn/shrimp powder or 100ml (3½oz) good-quality fish stock

coarsely ground black pepper, to taste

4-6 soft-boiled eggs, shelled and halved, to garnish

Put the goat meat in a large, heavy-based saucepan with the garlic, sugar, sea salt, paprika, turmeric and cornflour over a medium heat, stir well, cover and leave to steam in its own juices for 20 minutes or until the meat juices run clear. Set the meat aside and wipe out the pan.

Heat 1 tablespoon oil in the saucepan over a medium-high heat, add the meat in batches and cook until browned all over, adding another 1 tablespoon of oil to the pan to brown each batch. Remove from the pan and set aside in a bowl.

Add the remaining oil to the same pan, add half the onion and the ground hot pepper and sauté over a medium heat. Meanwhile, put the remaining onions, guinea pepper or grains of paradise, ginger and chillies in a blender or food processor and blend to a paste, then add to the frying onions. Reduce the heat slightly and cook, stirring continuously, for 3–4 minutes.

Stir in the tomato purée mixture and cook down the sauce for 10–12 minutes until it thickens to a paste and the mixture is reduced by approximately half.

Blend the tomatoes and peppers (if using) in the blender or food processor until smooth, then add to the pan along with the five-spice mix, crayfish or prawn/shrimp powder or fish stock and keep stirring until everything in the pot is blended together. Reduce the heat to low, cover and simmer for 25 minutes until the sauce is reduced and thickened.

Check for seasoning, adding black pepper to taste, then cook for a further 15 minutes, stirring regularly. As with Shito (hot pepper sauce – see page 228), the sauce should transform into a rich, dark colour.

Serve garnished with the soft-boiled eggs over Waakye Rice and a side of Simple Fried Plantain (see pages 162 and 42). The dish can be kept refrigerated in an airtight container for 3–5 days, but it won't last that long!

Ghana get Irish

★ There's nothing quite like an Irish–Ghanaian mash-up and these are some of my favourites.

Ghanaian-Irish Scotch Eggs

I spent many a summer eating 'the world's best black pudding' from Clonakilty in County Cork, Ireland, just down the road from my grandmother's in Bantry, and fresh free-range eggs from Shelia's farm next door.

SERVES 6

400g (14oz) Clonakilty black pudding

150g (5½oz) good-quality minced pork

100g (3½oz) Golden Mashed Yam (Oto; see page 35)

50g (1¾oz) fresh white breadcrumbs

1 tablespoon chopped parsley

1 teaspoon Ghanaian Five-spice Mix (see page 244)

½ Scotch Bonnet chilli, deseeded and diced (optional)

sea salt and freshly ground black pepper

6 eggs

500ml (18fl oz) sunflower oil, for deep-frying

COATING

100g (3½oz) cornflour seasoned with salt and pepper

½ teaspoon ground nutmeg

1–2 eggs, lightly beaten

150–200g (5½–7oz) gari (fermented, dried and ground cassava)

Mix the black pudding, pork, oto, breadcrumbs, parsley, spice mix and chilli, if using, together – this is a hands-on business, so get stuck in. Massage and knead the ingredients until evenly combined. Season well and then divide the meat mixture into 12 even-sized balls.

Add the eggs to a saucepan of boiling water and cook for 4–5 minutes for soft-boiled or 6–7 minutes for hard-boiled. Drain and place under cold running water until cool enough to handle, then shell.

You'll need plenty of work space for the next step. Flatten out each meat ball into a 7–8cm (2¾–3¼-inch) disc. Place a shelled egg in the centre of 6 of the discs, then top each with another disc. Mould the discs gently around the eggs until fully wrapped, ensuring that you seal all edges.

To coat the eggs, set up a mini factory line: the seasoned cornflour, with the nutmeg mixed in, in a bowl; the beaten egg in a second bowl, and the gari in a third bowl. First carefully roll an egg in the cornflour mixture, then dip into the beaten egg and finally roll in the gari to evenly coat. Set aside while you finish coating the rest of the eggs. Place the coated eggs in the fridge to firm up.

Heat the oil for deep-frying in a deep-fat fryer (the safest option) or heavy-based, deep saucepan filled to just under half the depth of the pan to 180°C (350°F). Lower 1–2 eggs into the hot oil at a time and fry for 5–7 minutes until golden all over, turning them regularly so that they cook evenly. Remove from the oil and drain on kitchen paper.

Leave to cool for 5 minutes before serving so that you don't burn your mouth when you tuck in. This is an insanely tasty beast of a Scotch egg!

Ghanaian-Irish Stew

Besides being one of mum's favourite dishes, this is one that Irish cookery traditionalists like to argue over – in particular, should it include vegetables or not? My mum used to add a whole array to hers as well as pearl barley. It must contain mutton or lamb – that's non-negotiable. The below incorporates Ghanaian ingredients and pleases both mum and dad when we get together for dinner.

SERVES 4

2 tablespoons vegetable oil

450g (1lb) boneless mutton or lamb shoulder, cut into 5cm (2-inch) chunks

1kg (2lb 4oz) yams, peeled and diced

115g (4oz) onion, roughly chopped

100g (3½oz) leeks, trimmed, cleaned and finely sliced

170g (6oz) carrots, peeled (if not organic) and roughly chopped

2 tablespoons cornflour

750ml (1⅓ pints) good-quality beef stock

5 guinea peppers, cracked open

ground or crushed cubeb pepper

1 Scotch Bonnet chilli, pierced

2 or 3 cabbage leaves, thinly sliced (optional)

sea salt, to taste

Preheat the oven to 160°C (325°F), Gas Mark 3.

Heat 1 tablespoon of the oil in a large frying pan, add half the mutton or lamb and cook until browned all over. Remove from the pan and place in a casserole dish. Cover with half the yam, onion, leeks and carrots.

Heat the remaining oil in the frying pan, add the remaining meat and brown all over as before. Add to the casserole and cover with the remaining vegetables.

Add the cornflour to the frying pan and stir really well to soak up any fat and juices. Cook over a gentle heat for 3 minutes, then add the stock a ladleful at a time, stirring continuously, until you have a thick, lump-free sauce. Add the guinea peppers and season with cubeb. Pour the sauce over the meat and vegetables and drop in the pierced Scotch Bonnet.

Add any remaining stock to the casserole, cover with a tight-fitting lid and cook in the oven for 1 hour.

Add the cabbage (if using), replace the lid and cook for a further hour. Check from time to time to make sure the stock isn't reducing too much. If necessary, add a little boiling water – the meat and vegetables should always be covered by liquid. If the sauce is too runny at the end, you can always cook it uncovered for a little longer.

Season to taste with sea salt and serve with a chunky slice of hard dough bread or a crusty loaf. Save some for tomorrow, when it will taste even better!

Steamed Mussels in Groundnut Broth

This is a play on two heavy-hitting classics: Nkatsenkwan (see page 150) and Irish steamed mussels. While you can't beat mussels fresh from Bantry Bay, any good-quality locally-sourced ones will do the trick.

SERVES 4 AS A MAIN, 6 AS A STARTER

1.8kg (4lb) fresh live mussels

6 tablespoons olive oil

8 shallots, thinly sliced

8 garlic cloves, thinly sliced

2 tablespoons coarse sea salt

300ml (½ pint) dry white wine

150–175ml (5–6fl oz) red wine

400ml (14fl oz) uncooked Chalé Sauce (see page 247)

4 small tomatoes, diced

50g (1¾oz) fresh root ginger, thinly sliced (unpeeled if organic)

500ml (18fl oz) good-quality vegetable stock

75g (2¾oz) parsley, chopped

150g (5½oz) roasted peanuts, crushed

2 Scotch Bonnet chillies, pierced

4 guinea peppers, cracked open

freshly grated Parmesan cheese, to serve (optional)

Scrub the mussels clean, pull away any beards and remove any barnacles. Discard any with damaged shells.

Place the mussels in a large bowl. If any are open, pinch them and, if they don't close, discard them.

Heat 3 tablespoons of the olive oil in a large saucepan, add the shallots, garlic and 1 tablespoon of the sea salt and sauté over a medium heat for a few minutes until soft.

Add the wine, chalé sauce, tomatoes and ginger and cook for 8–10 minutes until the tomatoes are tender and the mixture has thickened.

Add the mussels and all the remaining ingredients except the Parmesan, cover and cook for a further 3–4 minutes or until all the mussels have opened.

Remove the pan from the heat and discard any mussels that have failed to open. Spoon into large bowls, sprinkle with the Parmesan cheese if desired and serve.

Pictured overleaf, from left to right: Steamed Mussels in Groundnut Broth; Ghanaian-Irish Stew; Ghanaian-Irish Scotch Eggs.

★ Sides

Waakye Rice
Rice & Beans

★ In the Caribbean they have rice and beans, while in Ghana we have *waakye* (pronounced 'waa-che') rice – an incredibly popular breakfast and brunch. You can *see* people hurrying to work in the bustle of a steamy Accra morning firmly gripping a polythene bag of *waakye*. My Uncle Ernest dashes across the road every morning to get his before his household is even awake.

While *waakye* rice is simple enough to prepare, the dish is layered with a variety of sometimes complicated accompaniments, including the infamous Waakye Stew (*see* page 155 for my recipe); Simple Fried Plantain (*see* page 42); Shito (Hot Pepper Sauce; *see* page 228); spaghetti (or 'ta-lia', as it's commonly called roadside); small chop (salad); gari (fermented, dried and ground cassava); and an assortment of meat or fish.

The dried millet or sorghum leaves used to give waakye its characteristic reddish colour are reputed to offer considerable nutritional benefits and are gluten-free.

→ **TIPS** *Traditionally this dish is made by simply adding the rice to the pan of already boiling beans and leaves, but I prefer to remove as much of the starchiness from the beans as possible and add onions and fresh chilli.*

You can remove the leaves before serving, but I like to leave them in, as they give a dramatic flourish to the dish.

225–250g (8–9oz) dried black-eyed beans, or 400g (14oz) can organic black-eyed beans or red kidney beans

400g (14oz) medium- or long-grain brown rice

1 **tablespoon** coconut oil

1 onion, finely diced

3–4 dried millet or sorghum leaves, or 1 **teaspoon** bicarbonate of soda

1 red rocket (Anaheim) chilli, or bird's-eye chilli, thinly sliced

sea salt

1 **litre** (1¾ pints) boiling water, or good-quality chicken or vegetable stock

TO GARNISH (OPTIONAL)

2 soft-boiled eggs, shelled and halved

small bunch of chives, finely sliced

1 green chilli, finely sliced

I used to soak the beans for 3–4 hours in the traditional way, but who has time for that? You can just rinse the beans, place in a large saucepan, cover with water, bring to the boil, reduce the heat and simmer for at least 1 hour or until the beans are tender enough to be squeezed easily between thumb and forefinger. Drain and set aside. Faster still, use a can of beans – just drain, rinse and drain again.

Wash the rice in several changes of cold water until the water runs clear – I wash it at least 3 times – then drain.

Heat a large, heavy-based saucepan. Add the oil and onion and sauté over a medium heat for about 3 minutes or until lightly golden.

Meanwhile, wash the dried millet or sorghum leaves, if using – swiftly because the colour will start to run as soon as they get wet – and cut them into 7.5–10cm (3–4-inch) pieces.

Add the rice, beans, leaves, chilli and salt to the onions, tossing slightly. Stir in the measured water or stock (and the bicarbonate of soda, if using). Simmer, covered, for 15 minutes.

Turn off the heat. Leave to stand, covered, for 15 minutes until the water has been absorbed and the rice is tender.

Garnish with the soft-boiled eggs, chives and green chilli, if liked, and serve with shito as a side to any meat- or veg-based stew. It's also great with Kelewele (see page 44).

Bankye Totoe
Baked Cassava Fries

★ If you've ever eaten Peruvian food you will probably have tried cassava fries or chips – known there as yuka or manioc fries. Cassava is a tubular starchy root vegetable whose waxy, woody skin is a bit of a pain to peel, which is a shame because it's as diverse as yam as an alternative to potatoes. Luckily, you can now buy frozen cassava chunks that are peeled and ready to use, which cuts prep time by 75 per cent.

These baked cassava fries are a great alternative to the usual potato fries and chips, and you can enliven them further by adding a seasoning of your choice.

400g (14oz) cassava, prepped and peeled (see Tip, below)

cooking salt

2-3 tablespoons granulated sugar

4 garlic cloves, sliced

3 tablespoons chopped parsley

pinch of sea salt

cooking oil spray or vegetable oil, for coating

Jollof Relish or Shito Mayo (see pages 234 and 231), to serve

Cut the peeled cassava into basic chip shapes and rinse thoroughly in cold water to remove the starch. Place the chips in a saucepan, pour in water to just cover and add a little cooking salt and sugar.

Parboil the cassava chips for 10–15 minutes until just fork tender – if you overboil them, they will fall apart, so be vigilant!

Quickly drain the cassava chips and leave the steam to rise off the chips while they cool. Meanwhile, preheat the oven to 180°C (350°F), Gas Mark 4. Line a baking tray with foil or baking parchment.

Toss the cassava chips in the garlic, parsley, sea salt and a little cooking oil spray or vegetable oil in a bowl, coating evenly all over with the seasoning.

Spread the chips out on the lined baking tray in a single layer and bake for 30–40 minutes or until lightly browned and crisp at the edges, turning them over halfway through the cooking time. Serve warm with Jollof Relish or Shito Mayo.

→ **TIP** To prep cassava, cut off both ends and then cut in half lengthways. Remove the stalky thread running down through the middle of each half. Make a shallow cut into the skin of the cassava and gradually work your knife just under the pink layer of the cassava flesh to remove the skin.

MY GHANA STORY PART 3:

Jamestown - Accra's Wild, Wild South West

★ When I return from my travels in the Volta region, after having enjoyed a satisfying experience of acceptance and integration into the cookery skills of Ho kitchens, I am impatient to escape the hospitality chair and get closer to understanding the local cuisine.

'Jamestown is the real Accra,' according to my inside contact Redkat. Probably the oldest side of the city, its key landmarks are the lighthouse at its southernmost tip and then, as you move east along the coast, Fort James and Fort Ussher; neighbouring Ussher seamlessly blends into north Jamestown. Fort James is a busy harbour and hub of this community. These forts starkly mark the strongholds of slavery when the Gold Coast's stock trade was people.

Jamestown is a sprawling fishing community right on the Atlantic Coast of Accra and, at a time when the commercial focus seems to be moving inland, it's keeping Accra's port connections alive. It's a cluttered, open-sewered, jumbled, unaffected and glorious mess of a place to hang out – if you know the right people…

My Uncle Albert tries to discourage me from going in alone, or going in at all – 'It is full of hoodlums o' – but his disapproval only makes me more eager, though slightly cautious, being a light-skinned gay woman travelling alone. Redkat introduces me to a Jamestown resident called Emmanuel, who is to be my charming guide and, so it seems, my potential suitor for the day.

Yes, Jamestown is smelly, dirty and a warren, but it's a lively, connected community. Everyone knows Emmanuel and Emmanuel knows everyone. Once introduced as his 'wifey', I am made to feel welcome and those suspicious of an *obroni* with a camera relax and pose for portraits. (*Obroni* is supposed to mean foreigner – in practice it actually means white person – really used to describe anyone who has light skin, from what I can discern.)

Emmanuel leads me to a group of women who show me how they smoke fish on large wire racks. Another group demonstrates how they make kenkey in enormous vats with spoons made for, it seems, the hands of giants.

It is an industrious place with all industry geared towards food in one form or another – men pounding enough fufu to feed a small village; women tending smokers; children chasing goats that could later be their dinner. Every other hut or shack is selling, frying, smoking or gutting fish.

We are invited to an impromptu lunch and suddenly I am on a low stool, my knees up by my ears, eating prawns cooked on a makeshift wire barbecue over a coal bucket. We rip off heads, peel off shells and dip the curls of white flesh into some shito alongside a pot of coconut rice. We share a meal as perfect strangers and leave each other as if we might do it all again the next day.

After our greedily fast lunch we head to the beach – I want to go to a chop bar and Emmanuel obliges. Two scruffy scaffolding poles driven into the yellow sand support a wind-battered tarpaulin tied with fishing wire to what is little more than a hut on the beach. As my toes scratch through the sand towards it, I hear a transistor radio playing Ghanaian High-life music and the large, hand-painted, plywood sign that reads 'Chop Bar' comes into view. The smell of frying tilapia in ginger wafting through the air makes me pick up my pace.

Chop houses are not only the perfect place for the budget traveller, they are also a mainstay of the Ghanaian eating-out scene – essentially, 'chop' means 'eat'. These small canteens or roadside eateries are wonderfully simple places for good, thrifty, home-cooked food, sitting somewhere between a street-food cart and a restaurant. They have inspired both my restaurant and my street-food stalls, which we also call chop bars. Usually there will be a scattering of mismatched Formica-topped dining tables, plastic school chairs and even upturned oil drums for seating. Almost everything is served with fufu, banku or konkonte (ground and pounded cassava, corn/maize or groundnuts). If you're lucky, you'll be given a bowl of water in which to wash your hands.

The cook is a stout man with huge smiling eyes squashed into his round cheeks. I ask him what's good to eat, and joyfully he replies 'Everything!'. So I order the tilapia and a small bowl of hot pepper soup, now comfortable with having two lunches as well as three breakfasts. He laughs and tells me I need feeding. I ask if I can watch him cook. He glances over to Emmanuel as if to ask, why does this *obroni* woman want to watch me cook? Emmanuel says something in Twi and pushes me through the strips of plastic leading into the kitchen. My initiation begins.

Banku

★ Banku is like a giant dumpling made from fermented cornmeal porridge. It's a hugely popular accompaniment to soups and stews, and is always served with Whole Grilled Tilapia (see page 74).

When boiled it can be quite slimy, so it's not to everyone's taste, but if you're feeling adventurous (and strong), try making your own using the following recipe – it can be quite a meditative process. There is a wooden stick made specifically for preparing banku, but you can easily substitute an ordinary wooden spoon if you don't have one of those.

African or speciality grocery stores will stock both corn and cassava dough and they will also stock pre-packaged banku. It's also totally okay to buy ready-made banku – I usually do (see page 112 for my tips on buying banku).

275g (9¾oz) corn dough

140g (5oz) cassava dough

500ml (18fl oz) warm water, plus extra as required

½ teaspoon cooking salt, or to taste

Using clean hands, mix the corn dough and cassava dough together with the measured water in a large, heavy-based saucepan until it turns into a watery paste, then add the salt.

Using a banku stirring stick or wooden spoon, cook over a medium heat, stirring continuously, until it begins to thicken. You may need to add a little more water at this stage and keep stirring the mixture to prevent it from turning lumpy – be warned, it requires some elbow grease!

The banku will now continue to thicken and become stiff, and you need to keep vigorously kneading the dough-like mixture with the wooden stick or spoon against the side of the pan – more elbow grease!

Add a little water every now and then to soften your mixture, and after about 20 minutes you should have a dough that you can form into balls for serving. Note that banku is fairly heavy, so I recommend portions no bigger than the size of your fist, but it's completely up to you. Serve in balls with Ntroba Froe (Garden Egg & Okra Stew), Nkatsenkwan (Peanut Butter/Groundnut Stew with Lamb), or slice to serve with Whole Grilled Tilapia (see pages 147, 150 and 74). Any leftover banku can be wrapped in clingfilm and stored in the fridge for the next day.

★ This easy vegetable curry dip demonstrates how garden eggs can be just as versatile as regular aubergines. Serve as a tasty side dish with plain rice and side salads.

Garden Egg Dip

10 garden eggs, trimmed and quartered

sea salt

2 tablespoons olive oil

1 teaspoon cumin seeds

1 onion, thinly sliced

5cm (2-inch) piece fresh root ginger, finely grated (unpeeled if organic)

2 garlic cloves, very finely chopped

1 tablespoon curry powder

2 tomatoes, diced

110ml (3¾fl oz) natural low-fat yogurt

1 green bird's-eye chilli, finely chopped

½ bunch of coriander, finely chopped

Preheat the oven to 220°C (425°F), Gas Mark 7.

Place the garden eggs on a baking tray, season with a pinch of sea salt and drizzle with 1 tablespoon of the olive oil. Bake for 20–30 minutes until tender.

Remove from the oven and leave to cool, then peel away the skins if you prefer. Chop as you wish – the smaller you chop the garden eggs, the looser the dip will be. I sometimes leave them quite chunky as it looks pretty for serving to guests.

Heat the remaining 1 tablespoon of olive oil in a saucepan, add the cumin seeds and onion and sauté over a medium heat until the onion is tender. Stir in the ginger, garlic, curry powder and tomatoes and cook for 1 minute, then stir in the yogurt.

Mix in the chopped baked garden egg and chilli, and season to taste with sea salt. Cover the pan and cook over a high heat for 10 minutes.

Remove the lid, reduce the heat to low and continue cooking about 5 minutes. Serve sprinkled with the chopped coriander.

★ Coconut features hugely in the West African diet and every street corner will have someone selling fresh coconuts with a hole and a straw to sip from. Using fresh coconut to cook with is a dream but not always entirely practical, so good-quality organic canned coconut milk will suffice.

Coconut Rice

300–400g (10½–14oz) basmati or other long-grain white rice (75g/2¾oz per person is the norm but that's not enough in an African household, so I always go for at least 100g/3½oz per person, as you can always have seconds)

sea salt, to taste

400g (14oz) can organic coconut milk (you may not need it all)

Wash the rice thoroughly in cold water to remove as much starch as possible – I wash it in at least 3 changes of water until the water runs clear – then drain and place in a large, heavy-based saucepan. Pour in just enough water to cover the rice and add salt to taste – I use about ½ teaspoon sea salt, as I don't like over-salty rice. Cover and cook over a medium heat for about 5 minutes until it starts to boil – this allows the grains to open up.

Shake the can of coconut milk thoroughly before opening, then add about half the can to the rice and stir it through. Replace the lid and cook for a further 10 minutes over a medium-high heat.

Add another one-quarter of the can and stir it in, then reduce the heat and simmer for about 7 minutes until all the liquid has been absorbed and the rice is tender and fluffy.

→ **TIPS** You can serve the coconut rice in small bowls with any stew of your choice, such as Waakye Stew, Simple Beef Stew or Kontomire Froe (Beef & Spinach Stew; see pages 155, 137 and 130).

If you do have fresh coconut to hand, slice some slim shards a few centimetres long, lightly toast in a dry frying pan and use as a crunchy topping for the rice.

★ The strength and stamina required to make fufu from scratch could put it in to an Olympic sporting category! My uncle told me that a university in Accra tried to build a fufu-making machine but to operate it to replicate the pounding action was more hard work than just doing the action manually. If you ever get the chance, I do recommend having a go, but all-hail packet fufu for a simpler life!

Fufu

115g (4oz) plantain fufu flour

250ml (9fl oz) water, very warm or just boiled and slightly cooled

Put the flour in a small saucepan, mix in half of the measured water and stir into a thick paste.

Place the pan over a low heat and slowly add the rest of the water, stirring continuously and smoothing out any lumps with the back of a wooden spoon (the low heat will absorb the last of the moisture).

6

★ **Desserts**

★ In Ghana, nkatse cake or peanut brittle is a very common, popular street-food snack – my poor teeth suffer from coping with its sticky, chewy texture, but it's so tasty that it's worth it! Ordinarily this is made solely with roasted peanuts, but I like to use a variety of nuts to change it up a little. This recipe makes a great slab of the stuff that you can cut up into shards and serve with vanilla ice cream or just snack on when you fancy a treat.

MAKES ABOUT 550G
(1LB 4OZ)

Nkatse Cake
Peanut Brittle

butter or sunflower oil, **for greasing**

225g (8oz) caster sugar

125ml (4fl oz) water

50g (1¾oz) pistachio nuts, roughly chopped

50g (1¾oz) Spiced Cashews (see page 208), roughly chopped

50g (1¾oz) dry roasted peanuts, crushed

to serve

scoops of vanilla ice cream

juice of ½ lemon

Line a baking tray with greased nonstick baking parchment.

First make the caramel. Place the sugar in a heavy-based saucepan with the measured water and heat over a medium heat, stirring gently, until the sugar has dissolved and the mixture starts to boil. Now, stop stirring and leave the syrup to boil for a further 5–7 minutes before reducing the heat and simmering until it turns a deep brown caramel colour – you will need to pay close attention so that it doesn't burn.

Once the caramel is a good brown colour, remove the pan from the heat and – working quickly – stir through the chopped nuts, making sure they are evenly coated in the caramel.

Pour the caramel mixture into the lined tin. Using the back of a wooden spoon, spread the mixture out evenly and press it firmly into place until about 1cm (½ inch) thick. Take care because the mixture will be extremely hot.

Leave to cool completely before cutting up into shards. Serve with a scoop of vanilla ice cream and a squeeze of lemon juice, if you wish. Or place the shards in an airtight container to snack on later – stored in a cool, dry place they should keep for up to 1 week (if you can keep away from them for that long).

→ **TIP** Though it is such a simple recipe, making caramel requires your close attention!

★ This is a super-simple, earthy tasting shortbread recipe that combines sweet and savoury notes and smells like Christmas!

Cubeb Spiced Shortbread

125g (4½oz) butter, at room temperature, plus extra for greasing

55g (2oz) caster sugar

180g (6oz) plain flour, plus extra for dusting

1½ tablespoons Ghanaian Five-spice Mix (see page 244)

icing sugar, for sprinkling (optional)

Beat the butter and sugar together in a bowl until pale and fluffy.

Mix in the flour and spice mix until you have a smooth dough. Turn out on to a lightly floured work surface and gently roll out until the dough is 1cm (½ inch) thick.

Cut into bars with a knife, or into your desired shapes using cutters, and place on a greased baking tray. Sprinkle with icing sugar, if you like, and chill in the fridge for 20 minutes. Meanwhile, preheat the oven to 190°C (375°F), Gas Mark 5.

Bake for 15–20 minutes or until pale golden brown. Leave to cool on a wire rack and, if liked, sprinkle with icing sugar once cooled.

Leanne's Coconut Rice Pudding

★ My fiancée Leanne is a huge foodie and an excellent cook, heavily influenced by her travels across India and South East Asia, who loves helping me reinvent favourite dishes and test new recipes. Every time we go out for dinner, the discussion is always 'how could we do this differently?', and we came up with this recipe as a way of making the typical and simple Ghanaian breakfast dish of rice water – literally rice soaked in water – less watery and more exciting in flavour. In my grandma's house it's served with lashings of evaporated milk and sugar to make it taste interesting – an approach my dad also took to rice pudding at home. But our recipe uses lots of good, natural ingredients that will also soothe any sweet tooth – it's a real treat!

→ **TIP** You can also cook the rice pudding in a casserole dish or other covered ovenproof dish in an oven preheated to 180°C (350°F), Gas Mark 4 for the same length of time, removing the lid for the last 5 minutes to get a nice golden crisp topping.

150g (5½oz) pudding rice

400ml (14fl oz) can coconut milk

250ml (9fl oz) almond milk

3 **tablespoons** coconut sugar

1 **teaspoon** ground cinnamon

½ **teaspoon** ground nutmeg

TOPPING

1 **teaspoon** desiccated coconut, or thin shavings of fresh coconut

2 **teaspoons** coconut oil

1 **ripe** plantain or banana, peeled and thinly sliced

Place all the ingredients (except those for the topping) in a heavy-based saucepan and bring to the boil. Reduce the heat and simmer for 20–25 minutes, stirring occasionally to avoid sticking, until the liquid has been absorbed and the rice is cooked through.

For the topping, heat a small dry frying pan and toast the desiccated or fresh coconut for 1–2 minutes over a low heat so that it doesn't burn, then remove from the pan and set aside.

Add the coconut oil to the frying pan and then the plantain or banana slices and fry over a medium heat until lightly caramelized on both sides.

Serve the rice pudding in bowls topped with a sprinkle of the toasted coconut and fried plantain or banana slices.

★ The best of Ghana's fruit on a plate makes an ultra-simple yet fabulously colourful and deliciously sweet dessert. It also entails a fun trip to the market!

Ghanaian Fruit Salad

2 tablespoons fresh lime juice

2 tablespoons soft dark brown sugar

½ fresh pineapple, peeled, cored and cubed, or substitute **200-300g/7-10½oz canned** pineapple chunks if fresh is unavailable

2 sweet oranges, peeled and segmented

2 ripe mangoes, stoned, peeled and cubed

2 bananas, peeled and cut into slices 3cm (1¼ inches) thick

TO DECORATE

1 small green (unripe) papaya, deseeded and peeled (optional)

125g (4½oz) fresh coconut, thinly shaved and lightly toasted in a dry frying pan (see left for method)

Mix the lime juice and brown sugar together, then pour over the prepared fruits in a bowl. Cover the bowl with clingfilm and chill in the fridge for at least 1 hour.

If using the papaya, use a potato peeler to shave thin strips of the fruit, then drop them into a bowl of ice-cold water, which should prompt them to curl up into pretty strings.

Serve the fruit salad in bowls, decorated with the drained papaya shavings and the toasted coconut.

MY GHANA STORY PART 4: KANESHIE MARKET

★ Now buoyed up by my experiences of Ho and Jamestown and full of confidence, I am finally ready to spend some time on my own in the kitchen at Grandma's house. I have been challenged by Uncle Francis to make nkatsenkwan (groundnut soup/stew) and I need to go shopping.

I can see that Grandma is too frail to do anything in the kitchen. Her walking frame – she calls it her 'car' – is a necessity for moving her own 'Z'-bent frame, so her cooking lessons will have to be an oral history. I was therefore hoping that during this shopping adventure I could seduce Aunty Evelyn into teaching me some local dishes. She accepts the task like a peacock being courted by a duck.

Just a short tro-tro ride away from North Kanehsie, where I'm staying, Kaneshie Market is something else. When you arrive, the first thing that hits you is the smell. It's not altogether pleasant – a waft somewhere between rotting meat and a rubbish tip. A huge, multi-level, yellow 1970s construction is the centrepiece of the action, but it's surrounded on all sides by small colourful stalls and carts and general mayhem.

'Plenty fish o!' declares Evelyn, proudly shrugging her shoulders and adjusting her bag strap. I am too dumbstruck and stifled by the smell to respond – my brain is trying to tell my lungs that I don't need to inhale to stay alive while simultaneously telling my face not to screw up my nose.

Seafood seems to dominate the outside market – smoked herring, salmon, barracuda, cassava fish, red snapper, 'red fish', prawns, crabs of varying colours and sizes – it goes on spreading inwards along and across the vast ground floor before leading through to vegetables, shea butter and hair products. Decorative glass and wooden beads and household items – everything from toilet brushes to toothpicks – take up the second floor, with fabrics and tailoring on the third. All-in-all, this is a dark, cavernous ever-winding vault of local trade.

There is no ingredient to be found in local cooking (and beyond) that you can't buy here – plus it's a bit cheaper than other markets in central Accra, as it's very much a destination for locals rather than tourists. This is where the haggle happens and it's a real-deal African experience to be in the midst of it. You can hear Fante, Twi, Ga and Akan all clashing in the air from tongues moving as fast as money is exchanged, and it's as colourful as the local Ghana Cedi currency.

When we step back out of the cavern, the light is brutal and my unprepared nostrils once again sting with the acrid smell. I stumble and twist round to see who might have noticed – everyone around has of course, as I'm the only giant light-skinned lesbian there.

'Sorry o,' Evelyn says, in sympathy of my stumble but not my embarrassment, I imagine.

'What is that smell?' I say, trying not to hold my nose.

'What smell?' responds an impatient Evelyn.

'You can't smell it? It's like something rotting.'

'I don't smell it.'

Soon, we pass a stall with cows' legs upended – large, chunky limbs with hoofs pointing into the air like synchronized swimmers. Behind this are slabs of thick, off-white, almost nicotine-stained rubber. This is where the smell emanates from. Stringent and violent, it assaults my nasal hairs.

'It's that,' I say pointing. 'What is that?'

'Oh. That is Willy.'

'Willy? What's that?'

'Cowhide.'

'Really? You can eat that?'

'Oh, yes – you don't know Willy?' Evelyn is satisfied to point out something I've never seen or heard of. 'Let us get some. We can add it the groundnut. It makes it tasteful. Eh ehh.'

Up close, 'Willy' looks like pork belly or unroasted crackling but is much thicker and in this instance eminently smellier. I am quietly scared about adding it to my stew but say nothing, not wanting to prove myself a prissy foreigner after all. We choose some live land snails and I watch – inwardly horrified that this task is mine in a few hours – as the hawker demonstrates how to unleash them from their shell. She jabs a spear quickly through their oily-looking full flesh and twists them out... Over in seconds, but an image that persists in my mind for days.

We bruise our way through the busy tro-tro station and taxi rank and fight for our places in the share taxi, feeling quite different, I'm sure, about our respective bargains.

Our snails get home alive and go into the freezer box – alive 'to keep them fresh eh ehh'.

When you've had an over-indulgent week food-wise and really don't want to add to your guilt with a wicked pudding, this is the go-to dessert. I sometimes find that overtly healthy desserts aren't much fun to eat, but this recipe pairs Ghana's high-quality cocoa with the ever-versatile avocado for an ultra-simple and delicious treat that you can enjoy with a clear conscience!

Avocado & Divine Chocolate Mousse

1 ripe avocado

2 tablespoons Divine cocoa powder, plus extra as required

2 tablespoons agave nectar, or substitute honey, plus extra as required

90ml (6 tablespoons) almond milk, plus extra as required

25g (1oz) pistachio nuts, roughly chopped

purple edible flower, to decorate (optional)

Cut the avocado in half lengthways, then slightly twist the halves to separate them. Holding the avocado half containing the stone firmly and carefully on a chopping board, chop the heel of the knife into the stone and lift it out. Cut through the flesh of each half into large cubes, then turn the skin inside out and gently scoop the cubed flesh into a blender.

Add the cocoa, agave nectar and almond milk and blend until smooth. If you've used a larger avocado and the mixture seems a little too thick, add an extra tablespoonful or so of almond milk. Taste and add an extra teaspoonful of agave or cocoa if necessary.

Spoon the mixture equally between 2 glass tumblers and chill in the fridge for at least an hour.

To serve, sprinkle with the chopped pistachios and decorate with a lovely little edible flower if you're feeling fancy.

→ **TIPS** This is an easy recipe to multiply up for serving 4 or more people.

Divine sustainably and ethically farm their chocolate in Ghana, so do source their cocoa powder if you can.

★ Plantain, chocolate, nuts...This is a killer combo – so moreish, so easy!

Divine Chocolate-covered Plantains

2 large ripe plantains, peeled and sliced into rounds

pinch of sea salt

125g (4½oz) 70% Divine dark chocolate, broken into pieces

50g (1¾oz) pistachio nuts, chopped

Preheat the oven to 160°C (325°F), Gas Mark 3. Line a baking tray with greaseproof paper.

Lay out the plantain slices on the lined tray, sprinkle with the sea salt and roast for 10–15 minutes until they start to crisp. Remove the baking tray from the oven and leave the roasted plantain slices to cool.

Meanwhile, put the chocolate in a heatproof bowl set over a saucepan of barely simmering water and leave until melted.

Dip the roasted plantain slices into the melted chocolate to coat just half of the surface. Lay the dipped slices out on a sheet of baking parchment and sprinkle the chocolate with the chopped pistachios before leaving to dry. Serve straight away.

→ **TIP** *Try sprinkling the melted chocolate with toasted desiccated coconut for a sweeter, crunchy result.*

★ There isn't much you can't do with plantain, and when it's super-ripe it's great for transforming into desserts and baking. If, like me, cake making isn't your greatest talent, this is about as simple as it gets to cook up a loaf cake.

Honey & Plantain Ginger Cake

200g (7oz) unsalted butter at room temperature, diced, plus extra for greasing

2 large very ripe plantains, peeled and diced, plus extra, sliced, to decorate

200ml (7fl oz) clear honey

225ml (8fl oz) buttermilk

2 large eggs, beaten

1cm (½-inch) piece fresh root ginger, grated (unpeeled if organic), optional

1 tablespoon Ghanaian Five-spice Mix (see page 244)

1½ teaspoons baking powder

1 teaspoon cooking salt

1 teaspoon vanilla extract

340g (11¾oz) plain flour

Preheat the oven to 180°C (350°F), Gas Mark 4. Grease a large loaf tin.

Combine all the ingredients except the flour in a large mixing bowl and beat together thoroughly.

Sift in the flour about 50g (1¾oz) at a time, mixing well after each addition.

Pour the mixture into the loaf tin and decorate the top with overlapping slices of plantain. Bake for 50 minutes–1 hour.

Leave to cool in the tin, or transfer to a wire rack to cool. Serve warm or cold. The cake will keep fresh in an airtight container for up to 2 days.

★ Bofrot is the famous Ghanaian doughnut, a popular street food that comes wrapped in newspaper. Traditionally, palm wine is used in place of yeast, but it's harder to come by than yeast, so I have used the latter here but with the addition of white wine. The doughnuts are still really tasty if you prefer to leave the wine out – just replace the liquid with extra warm water.

Bofrot
Puff Puff

40g (1½oz) caster sugar, plus 50g (1¾oz) for coating

cooking salt

2½ teaspoons fast-action dried yeast

100ml (3½fl oz) warm water

2-4 teaspoons white wine

½ egg, beaten

70g (2½oz) strong white flour, sifted

45g (1½oz) plain flour, sifted

¼ teaspoon baking powder

1 tablespoon ground nutmeg

½ teaspoon ground cinnamon, plus 30g (1oz) for coating

1 teaspoon vanilla extract (optional)

500ml (18fl oz)–1 litre (1¾ pints) vegetable oil, for deep-frying

Mix the sugar, ½ teaspoon salt, the yeast, measured warm water and wine together in a large bowl and leave to stand for 5 minutes, during which time bubbles should begin to appear as the yeast starts working.

At this point, add the beaten egg, then gradually mix in the flours, baking powder, spices, vanilla extract (if using) and a pinch more salt and mix together well.

Cover the bowl with clingfilm and leave to rise in a warm place for 1–2 hours or until the batter has doubled in size.

Heat the oil in a deep-fat fryer (the safest option) or heavy-based, deep saucepan filled to just under half the depth of the pan to 160°C (325°F). Test the temperature of the oil with a small drop of the batter – it should slowly rise to the surface and brown slowly.

Drop a few separate tablespoonfuls of the batter into the hot oil and fry for 2 minutes or until golden brown, then turn each bofrot over and fry until evenly dark golden brown all over. Remove with a slotted spoon and drain on kitchen paper. Repeat with the remaining batter.

Mix the extra sugar and cinnamon together on a deep plate, then roll the bofrot around the plate to coat them in the mixture. Serve warm or at room temperature on their own – or with clotted cream if you have it!

→ **TIPS** Dip your tablespoon for adding the batter to the fryer in the hot oil, to prevent the mixture sticking to it.

If the doughnuts don't keep their shape when deep-fried, there is probably too much liquid in your batter, and if they brown on the outside before cooking through on the inside, the oil is probably too hot.

★ I am the first to admit that I'm not a great baker, so when it comes to desserts I like foolproof. This gooey cake is great for guaranteeing your way to pudding success and I love the fact that it incorporates cassava. This is one for when you're feeling indulgent, as it's naughty as hell!

Coconut & Cassava Cake

sunflower oil, **for greasing**

500g (1lb 2oz) cassava

4 eggs, 2 separated

307g (10½oz) can condensed milk

400ml (14fl oz) can coconut milk

half a 410g (14½oz) can evaporated milk

150g (5½oz) soft light brown sugar

75g (2¾oz) desiccated coconut

Preheat oven to 160°C (325°F), Gas Mark 3. Grease two rectangular baking tins about 20 x 30cm (8 x 12in) and 2.5cm (1in) deep.

Peel the cassava (see Tip on page 192), rinse thoroughly in cold water to remove the starch and pat dry, then grate finely into a large mixing bowl.

Place 2 whole eggs and 2 egg whites in a bowl and beat together. Place the 2 egg yolks in a separate bowl.

For the topping, add one-third of the can of condensed milk and two-thirds of the can of coconut milk to the egg yolks and beat together well.

Add all the remaining ingredients (except the egg yolk mixture) to the cassava bowl and mix together well, making sure you add the remaining condensed milk and coconut milk from the cans. Pour the mixture into the greased tins and bake for 30–40 minutes or until there is no liquid on top.

Remove the cakes from the oven and spread the topping mixture evenly over both cakes, then increase the oven temperature to 180°C (350°F), Gas Mark 4 and bake for a further 20–30 minutes until they start to brown a little and the liquid has disappeared.

Leave the cakes to cool completely in the tins before serving. They will keep in the fridge for up to 3 days.

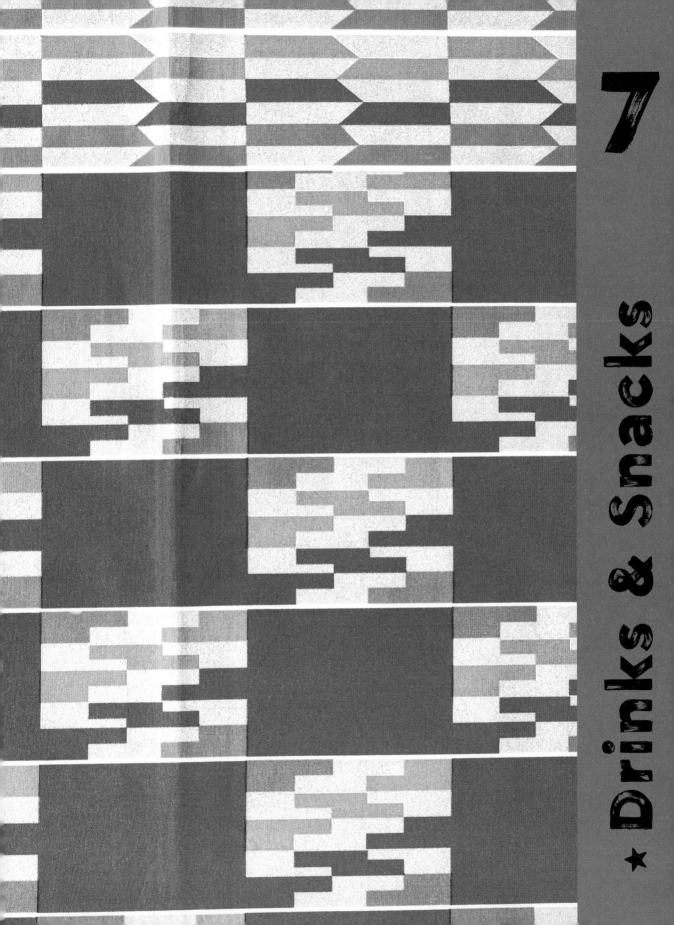

7

★ Drinks & Snacks

★ Bankye is the indigenous name for cassava and *Kaklo* means fried – so you will notice these words throughout the recipes individually where a dish has a traditional name. Agbeli is the specific Fante name for cassava, hence Agbeli Kaklo. Made from grated cassava, this is one of Ghana's favourite savoury snacks and has a wonderful crunch and texture. They are often eaten with grated or shaved fresh coconut.

AGBELI KAKLO
Bankye (Cassava) Dumplings

2–3 cassava

500ml–1 litre (18fl oz–1¾ pints) vegetable oil, for deep-frying

1 onion, finely chopped or grated (depending on the texture you would like)

sea salt, to season

2–3 red rocket (Anaheim) chillies, finely chopped, plus extra for serving (optional)

1 egg, beaten

fresh coconut, sliced or grated into thin shavings, to serve

Wash and peel the cassava (see Tip on page 192), cut each down the middle lengthways so that you can remove the stalky thread running through it, then grate on the smallest holes of a grater.

Place the grated cassava in a sieve and rinse thoroughly in cold water to remove the starch. Leave to drain. If necessary, gather the cassava up in a piece of muslin and squeeze out any excess moisture. Leave to air-dry a little while you heat the oil for deep-frying in a deep-fat fryer (the safest option) or heavy-based, deep saucepan filled to just under half the depth of the pan to 180–190°C (350–375°F) or until a cube of bread browns in 30 seconds.

Add the onion and sea salt along with the chillies, if using, to the grated cassava and mix well before combining with the beaten egg. Form the mixture into plum-sized balls, pressing firmly together to bind.

Fry the balls, in batches, turning intermittently to cook them evenly. Once the balls bob to the top and are a nice golden colour all over they are ready – this should take a few minutes per batch. Remove from the pan and drain on kitchen paper.

Serve warm with the fresh coconut and chilli slices, if using.

★ Kale is certainly a delicious and healthy green, but there is nothing especially Ghanaian about it. So why is this recipe included, you may ask? Well, I used to make this dish as a garnish for my Simple Grilled Mackerel and Pan-fried Tilapia Fillets with Spiced Baobab Butter (see pages 83, 82 and 232), and customers kept saying that it was so tasty and moreish that a garnish just wasn't enough and it should be served as a side. The customer is always right, so I duly added it to the menu and it has proven very popular ever since – thank you, customers!

Crispy Fried Kale

250ml (9fl oz) vegetable oil, for deep-frying

1 whole head of curly kale, about 150–200g (5½–7oz) (see Tips, below)

1 tablespoon sea salt

100g (3½oz) Kelewele Dry Spice Mix (see page 245)

Heat the oil in a deep-fat fryer (the safest option) or heavy-based, deep saucepan filled to just under half the depth of the pan to 180–190°C (350–375°F) or until a cube of bread browns in 30 seconds. Have a lid to hand, as you will need to cover the pan as soon as you drop the kale in.

Break the separate leaf stems away from the central stalk. Using a knife or scissors, trim off the woody ends of the leaf stems and, if necessary, cut the kale at its various stem points into separate pieces of around 4–5cm (1½–2 inches) in length.

Wash the kale in a colander and leave it to drain thoroughly. If necessary, shake off the water and pat the leaves dry with kitchen paper – when frying, the kale will cause the hot oil to splutter in any case, but excess water will make the reaction more violent and dangerous!

Once the oil is hot enough, use a pair of tongs to lower 1–2 pieces of kale into the oil. Put the lid on immediately, or hover your lid over the top of the pan to minimise the risk of hot oil spitting back at you! The kale really just needs to be dunked, so remove with tongs after 20–30 seconds to a tray lined with kitchen paper.

Repeat with the remaining kale, and once drained, you should have some very crispy kale! Transfer to a dish, sprinkle over the salt and toss to coat, then sprinkle over the spice mix. Serve warm or at room temperature.

→ **TIPS** You can use bags of sliced kale but it shrinks when fried and therefore soaks up more oil, so I recommend buying whole heads of kale — and it's cheaper anyway!

You can also bake the kale in an oven preheated to 180–200°C (350–400°F), Gas Mark 4–6 for a few minutes — lightly baste the kale in olive oil before placing on a baking tray.

★ Walking through Jamestown, down by the harbour in Accra, your senses are overwhelmed by the sheer quality of fish frying and smoking over large pits and grills. Smoking fish is a commonly used method of preserving the shelf life of the great daily hauls and mackerel is most common of all. The deep, earthy notes of smoked mackerel make it great for underpinning many stews such as Fetri Detsi (see page 135), and in its most simple form it makes a fantastic snack or appetiser.

Spiced Mackerel Pâté

300g (10½oz) skin-on smoked mackerel fillets

75g (2¾oz) crème fraîche

juice of 1 lemon

1 tablespoon ground grains of paradise, or substitute **½ teaspoon** ground mace and **½ teaspoon** ground nutmeg

1 teaspoon coarsely ground black pepper

sea salt flakes

small bunch of chives, finely chopped

handful of Spiced Cashews (see page 208), roughly chopped for topping

hard dough loaf, or substitute brioche, to serve

Remove the skin from the smoked mackerel fillets and flake the fish into small pieces in a bowl, removing any stray bones.

Add the crème fraîche, lemon juice, grains of paradise and black pepper. Using a fork, mash the mixture together until you're happy with the consistency and season with salt to taste.

Stir in the chives and top with the spiced cashews.

Just before serving, preheat the oven to 180°C (350°F), Gas Mark 4. Thinly slice the hard dough loaf, spread the slices on a baking tray, drizzle with a little oil and sprinkle with sea salt flakes. Bake for 5–7 minutes, until toasted and golden.

Serve the pâté with the toast on the side.

★ Okra, also known as ladies' fingers in Indian or Caribbean cooking, is very common in Ghanaian cooking and is called *nkruma*. As a child I used to hate it – my experience was always that of an over-cooked, slimy mush. After some research, I discovered it is the silken pods inside that create the mucilage in cooked okra – so the less you cut into the tiny seed pods, the less slimy it will be. The trick with okra is to try to retain its crunch (see Ntroba Froe/Garden Egg & Okra Stew, page 147).

SERVES 4-6
AS A SIDE

Nkruma Pan-fried Okra

500g (1lb 2oz) okra

5cm (2-inch) piece fresh root ginger, finely grated (unpeeled if organic)

2 garlic cloves, very finely chopped

1 red rocket (Anaheim) chilli or 1 tablespoon dried chilli flakes

¼ teaspoon sea salt

¼ teaspoon coarsely ground black pepper

grated zest and juice of 1 lime

2 tablespoons rapeseed oil or olive oil (I prefer to use organic rapeseed oil for light frying)

Using a sharp knife, trim the tail off each okra pod, then cut in half lengthways and add to a bowl. Add all the remaining ingredients with 1 tablespoon of the oil and mix together well. Cover the bowl with clingfilm and leave to marinate in the fridge until you're ready to cook – preferably up to 1 hour but 15 minutes will do.

Heat the remaining 1 tablespoon of oil in a shallow frying pan and fry the okra, in batches, over a medium heat – you just want to lightly char the okra and maintain its crunch, so a few minutes, turning occasionally, should do it. Remove the cooked okra from the pan and, if serving as is, keep hot while you fry the remaining batches.

Serve hot as a side dish, or leave to cool while you make your batter for the Nkruma (Okra) Tempura (see below).

· ·

★ This is an easy way to jazz up okra and makes a great beer snack or pre-dinner appetizer with a little extra sea salt shaken over them at the end.

SERVES 4-6
AS A SIDE

Nkruma (Okra) Tempura

1 quantity marinated okra (see Pan-fried Okra, above)

BATTER

150g (5½oz) plain flour

1 teaspoon ground nutmeg

pinch each of sea salt and freshly ground black pepper

200-250ml (7-9fl oz) soda water (if you have it, otherwise tap water is fine)

500ml-1 litre (18fl oz-1¾ pints) vegetable oil, for deep-frying

To make the batter, mix the flour, nutmeg and seasoning together in a bowl, then beat in the soda water.

Heat the oil for deep-frying in a deep-fat fryer (the safest option) or heavy-based, deep saucepan filled to just under half the depth of the pan to 160–180°C (325–350°F). Divide your marinated okra into 5 or 6 equal portions, then coat each portion evenly in the batter.

Deep-fry each portion at a time for about 2 minutes or until golden and crispy. Remove from the oil, drain on kitchen paper and keep hot while you fry the remaining batches. Serve as a delicious snack or side.

→ **TIP** *You can substitute gluten-free flour for the plain flour.*

Akara/Koose
Black-eyed Bean Fritters

★ These delicious bean paste fritters go by the names of *akara* or *koose* in Ghana and are known variously in West Africa as *kose*, *accara* and *kosai*. Akara is commonly eaten as a snack or breakfast food, but it has many variations and, as with much of West African food, it has travelled well. In New Orleans, these fritters are known as *calas*, in Brazil as *acaraje* and Barbados as *pumpjin accra*. Nigeria has some great variations, too, such as *kara egusi* (*egusi* or *agushi* being a type of melon seed).

400g (14oz) can organic black-eyed beans

1 red onion, finely diced

1 egg, lightly beaten

100g (3½oz) okra, trimmed and finely sliced, or use cored, deseeded and diced peppers

½ Scotch Bonnet chilli, deseeded and finely chopped

1 tablespoon cayenne pepper

1 small red chilli, finely diced (optional)

sea salt, to taste

225ml (8fl oz) water

500ml–1 litre (18fl oz–1¾ pints) sustainable palm oil, carotene oil or coconut oil, for deep-frying

Drain the can of beans, rinse and drain again.

Add the beans to a blender or food processor and blend until smooth, adding a little water to loosen the mixture as necessary.

Tip the blended beans into a large bowl, add the remaining ingredients (except the water and oil) and mix together well.

Gently whisk the mixture with a fork, allowing air to circulate through the mixture – this creates a fluffy rather than a stodgy mixture – while gradually adding just enough water until the mixture gently drops off a spoon.

Heat the oil for deep-frying in a deep-fat fryer (the safest option) or heavy-based, deep saucepan filled to just under half the depth of the pan to 180–190°C (350–375°F) or until a cube of bread browns in 30 seconds. Lower separate tablespoonfuls of the mixture into the hot oil, a few at a time, and fry until golden. The balls should gently turn over by themselves in the hot oil, but if not, move them around so that they fry evenly – it should take just a few minutes until they are nicely browned. If the balls sink to the bottom of the pan, the oil isn't hot enough, and if they brown immediately without having time to cook through to the centre, the oil is too hot.

Remove from the oil, drain on kitchen paper and leave to cool slightly before serving warm, or leave to cool completely and chill before serving. The great thing about akara is that you can eat them alone as a tasty snack, or serve chilled with a dip, or as a side dish with a stew.

→ **TIPS** *It helps to oil the spoon that you're using to drop the mixture into the oil.*

Chilling the bean paste mixture in the fridge for an hour will firm the mixture up and reduce the risk of the fritters falling apart while frying.

You can add a little rice flour or cornflour to the mixture if it's too wet.

★ Nuts are a good protein-packed snack. Groundnuts, in particular, are very common throughout Ghana and are eaten with bananas, Iced Kenkey (*see page 218*) and Kelewele (*see page 44*). Here, I've just roasted some cashews and added a little spice to give them a great kick and robustness that takes them from boring to boom as a pre-dinner appetizer or party snack.

MAKES 400G
(14OZ)

Spiced Cashews

400g (14oz) raw or roasted cashew nuts

2 teaspoons groundnut oil

2 teaspoons smoked paprika

2 teaspoons ground cumin

sea salt, for sprinkling

Preheat the oven to 190°C (375°F), Gas Mark 5.

Mix all the ingredients except the salt together in a bowl, then spread out on a baking tray and roast for 12–15 minutes until the nuts are crisp and lightly browned, giving the tray a shake halfway through the cooking time.

Remove from the oven and sprinkle with sea salt. Leave to cool, then store in an airtight container. Use within a month.

★ Cassava is a robust root vegetable that can be cooked in many similar ways to yam or potatoes. This is a super-simple way to adapt an ordinary vegetable into a palate party.

Spiced Cassava Patties

450g (1lb) cassava

1 **small** red onion, grated or very finely chopped

1 **bunch** of spring onions, finely diced

1 egg, beaten

2 **tablespoons** plain flour

1 garlic clove, crushed

1 **tablespoon** chopped thyme

1 **tablespoon** ground turmeric

2 **small** red chillies, finely chopped (optional)

sea salt and freshly ground black pepper

rapeseed oil or olive oil, for shallow-frying

Peel the cassava (see my Tip for preparing cassava on page 164), rinse thoroughly in cold water to remove the starch and pat dry, then grate into a bowl.

Add the red onion, spring onions and egg, then stir in the flour. Add all the remaining ingredients except the oil and mix in.

Form the cassava mixture into 8 patties about 2cm (¾inch) thick.

Heat a little oil in a large, nonstick frying pan, add the patties and fry over a medium-high heat for about 3–4 minutes until golden at the edges, then flip over and fry until golden brown on the other side. Serve hot with Jollof Relish (see page 234) for a light lunch, or as a side with a main dish.

★ I adore Shito (Hot Pepper Sauce) and can eat it by the spoonful on its own, but it's also incredibly versatile and can be used in many different ways.

This is yet another way of using it, to make a very moreish pre-dinner snack that leaves a small ball of fire in your mouth, but somehow you can't stop going for the next one – it's my new favourite party snack!

Shito Parcels

250–300ml (9–10fl oz) vegetable oil, for deep-frying

1 sheet filo pastry

10–15g (¼–½oz) butter

50–75g (1¾–2¾oz) Shito (Hot Pepper Sauce; see page 228) per sheet of filo

Heat the oil in a deep-fat fryer (the safest option) or heavy-based, deep saucepan filled to just under half the depth of the pan to 190–200°C (375–400°F) or until a cube of bread browns in 30 seconds – leave to heat over a medium-high heat so that it's hot enough for frying once you've prepared the parcels.

Lay out a damp muslin on a large chopping board or a sanitized work surface. Carefully remove a sheet of filo at a time – they crack very quickly when exposed to the air, so make sure you return any filo to the packet that you're not using at the time. This can be a bit fiddly, but it's better than wasting your filo. Lay the filo sheet out flat in a landscape position on top of the muslin and brush it evenly with the melted butter.

Take 1 heaped teaspoon of shito and spread it in a column about 1cm (½ inch) wide down the length of the filo sheet from top to bottom, as evenly as you can. Repeat across the sheet, leaving a 2cm (¾-inch) space between each column of shito.

Using a sharp knife, carefully cut down in between each column of shito you've drawn and then gently but firmly roll the strips of filo lengthways into tubes. Cut each tube of filo into 3–4cm (1¼–1½-inch) pieces and set aside in a bowl or on a plate. It doesn't matter too much if they're not especially neat, but they must be sealed at the edges so that the shito doesn't leak out when frying, so you may need to press the edges between finger and thumb or use an extra brush of butter.

Repeat with more filo sheets, or until you have made the quantity you need.

Check that the oil is hot enough by gently lowering a parcel on a slotted spoon into the oil – it should float and start to crisp almost immediately. Deep-fry the parcels, in batches, for 1–2 minutes. Remove from the pan and drain on kitchen paper. Serve hot straight away, or leave to cool for a while and serve just warm.

Moringa Makeovers

★ Moringa! Once again an indigenous West African superfood that is breaking ground in the well-being and health-food markets. It has been championed in particular by Aduna World, who are working very closely with local Ghanaian producers to create sustainable methods of farming and production, where Ghanaians actually get to reap the rewards of their labour and build profitable farming communities – go Aduna! Go moringa!

What is Moringa?

The mighty *Moringa oleifera* tree is sometimes described as the 'miracle tree' or 'drumstick tree'. Its small, round leaves can be harvested all year round and are crammed full of nutrition, including protein, calcium, beta-carotene, vitamin C, essential amino acids, potassium and so much more.

The health benefits of moringa are numerous but it has a very earthy taste, akin to nutty spinach and reminiscent of kelp, spirulina and other similar green superfoods, and therefore is not a great palate pleaser on its own. So here are a few ways in which you can incorporate moringa into your diet to boost your immune system and give your day a feel-good factor without having to hit the gym.

BREAKFAST

Add just 1 teaspoon of moringa powder to your porridge oats and watch it swirl deep green with goodness, or add ½ teaspoon to your spinach omelette or scrambled eggs to give yourself a double boost of lutein (a carotenoid and powerful antioxidant naturally present in both eggs and moringa).

JUICES & SMOOTHIES

Just ½ teaspoon of moringa powder added to your juice or smoothie will give it a noticeable kick, adding 1 tablespoon of clear honey or agave syrup will help to disguise the bitter leafy taste while maintaining a healthy glass of goodness. This works incredibly well with any avocado-based smoothie to get that moringa morning feeling.

SALAD

Add a light sprinkling of moringa over any salad – you won't notice it, but your body will!

★ A few moringa recipes to get your imagination flowing:

Moringa Tea

You can add moringa powder to hot water to create a super-nutritious well-being tea. It's important not to boil or cook moringa because it will lose its health properties, but added to pre-boiled water and brewed for a few minutes you've got a wake-up call to get you set for the day. The strong, bitter taste of moringa can be masked by adding honey or, better still, agave syrup.

SERVES 1

½ **teaspoon** moringa powder

125ml (4fl oz) hot water

1 teaspoon agave syrup

Stir the moringa powder into the measured hot water until dissolved, then add the agave syrup to sweeten.

Moringa Mojito

A mojito has to be one of my favourite summer cocktails. With a dash of moringa added, you will probably stop at one or two because it will have you bouncing with energy!

SERVES 1

1½ limes, 1 juiced, ½ sliced into thin wedges

2–3 teaspoons agave syrup, or substitute caster sugar

12 mint leaves, plus 1 extra sprig, to garnish

½ teaspoon moringa powder

ice cubes

4 tablespoons dark rum

75–100ml (2½–3½fl oz) soda water, for topping up

Using a pestle or the back of a spoon, gently bash the lime wedges with the agave syrup in a glass to extract the flavour and aroma of the lime.

Add the mint leaves and moringa powder to the glass and gently mash together with the lime wedges and agave.

Add a few ice cubes to the glass. Then separately crush some ice cubes to top up the glass until it is nearly half full.

Add the rum and stir with a long spoon until everything is well combined.

Top up the glass with the soda water and stir again. Add extra ice, if desired, garnish with a sprig of mint and serve.

Moringa Pesto

Of course pesto *should* contain pine nuts and a nice creamy expensive cheese such as pecorino Romano or Parmigiano Reggiano – in Italy you couldn't call it a pesto without these key ingredients. Even so, this adaptation of the traditional recipe into a spicy, super-healthy, vegan pesto in which the unique nutty spinach flavour of moringa is perfectly balanced may make you change your perception about what pesto can be.

MAKES 450–500ML (16–18FL OZ)

2 garlic cloves, peeled

1 green Scotch Bonnet or habanero chilli, deseeded

300–350g (10½–12oz) Spiced Cashews (see page 208)

140g (5oz) wild rocket

juice of ½ lemon

1–2 teaspoons moringa powder

125ml (4fl oz) extra virgin olive oil or cold-pressed rapeseed oil

½ teaspoon sea salt

½ teaspoon freshly ground black pepper

basil leaves, to garnish

Throw everything except half the oil, the sea salt, black pepper and basil into a blender and blend to a coarse paste.

Add the sea salt and black pepper to the mixture and pulse while slowly adding the remaining oil.

Toss this spicy, creamy power pesto with the basil leaves and any cooked pasta of your choice, or thin with extra oil to use as a salad dressing.

Sobolo
Sorrel Juice

★ This is an incredibly refreshing drink made from the vibrant dried flowers of the red sorrel plant, which is reputed to offer many health benefits including reducing blood pressure and calming nerves. The flowers have a sharp-sour punch, but the juice from the petals once sweetened with sugar resembles cranberry juice. This drink is ideal for summertime parties and can be livened up further by the addition of vodka to turn it into a sorrel cocktail.

150–200g (5½–7oz) dried red sorrel (hibiscus flowers)

10 whole cloves

200g (7oz) stem ginger, roughly grated or thinly sliced

2–3 guinea peppers, cracked open (optional)

1 star anise

110ml (3¾fl oz) lemon juice

1.5 litres (2¾ pints) water

200g (7oz) demerara or soft dark brown sugar, or to taste

ice cubes, to serve

TO GARNISH

sprigs of mint

lime **wedges**

Lightly rinse the sorrel petals to remove any grit – the colour will run, which you don't want to lose, so be quick.

Place all the ingredients except the sugar in a large, deep saucepan – the mixture may bubble up, so a deep pan is necessary to avoid the mixture overflowing. Bring to the boil and boil for about 20 minutes or until the petals have given up all their colour.

Remove from the heat, cover and leave to steep for at least 5 hours, preferably overnight.

Strain the mixture into a jug and stir in the sugar to taste. Serve over ice, garnished with a sprig of mint and wedges of lime.

→ **TIP** *Try sobolo in my Hot Gin Punch (see page 222).*

★ Since there is such an abundance of wonderful exotic fruits sold roadside in Ghana, it's super-easy to whizz up some great smoothies.

SERVES 2

Mango & Lime Smoothie

2 ripe mangoes, stoned, peeled and chopped

juice of 2 limes

2 × 120g (4½oz) pots natural yogurt

600ml (1 pint) apple juice

Put all the ingredients in a blender and blend until smooth. Serve in chilled glasses.

→ **TIP** *Replace the yogurt with 3 ripe bananas for a thick, dairy-free option.*

★ Remember Ovaltine? Milo is a bit like it, having a malty chocolatey flavour. It's ubiquitous in Ghana and hard to miss in any case with its strikingly bright green packaging. A bit naughty but ever so tasty, Mum used to turn Milo into milkshakes for us in the summer, which my sister and I slurped down, so this is a nostalgic nod to those happy days.

SERVES 1

Milo Milkshake

225ml (8fl oz) fresh milk, chilled

4 heaped teaspoons Milo powder, plus an extra 1 teaspoon for dusting

1–2 scoops organic vanilla or chocolate ice cream

5 ice cubes

2 teaspoons finely ground nuts or Spiced Cashews (see page 208), for topping (optional)

Put the milk, Milo, ice cream and ice cubes in a blender and blend together until smooth.

Pour into a tall glass. Dust with the extra Milo powder and top with the nuts, if you like.

★ There's a well-known soft drink brand that have turned a pretty penny out of the humble African kola nut. For an organic and natural version of that well-loved beverage, you need look no further than below.

Bese
Homemade Kola

2 tablespoons chopped kola nuts

225ml (8fl oz) water

grated zest of about 8 limes

200g (7oz) granulated sugar

2 tablespoons lime juice

¼ teaspoon vanilla extract

soda water, for diluting

CARAMEL SYRUP

135g (4¾oz) granulated sugar

75ml (5 tablespoons) water

4 allspice berries

1 cinnamon stick, lightly crushed

55ml (4 tablespoons) boiling water

First make the caramel syrup. Place all the ingredients except the measured boiling water in a small, heavy-based saucepan and bring to the boil over a high heat, stirring occasionally to dissolve the sugar. Reduce the heat to medium and continue to cook, again stirring occasionally, for 10–12 minutes until the mixture reaches 190°C (375°F) or it turns deep brown – you need to keep a watchful eye to prevent the mixture solidifying.

As soon as the mixture turns dark brown, remove the pan from the heat, stir in the boiling water and set aside to cool.

Place the kola nuts and measured water in a separate small saucepan and bring to a simmer over a medium-high heat. Reduce the heat to medium and simmer gently for 10–15 minutes.

Using your fingers, rub the lime zest into 2 tablespoons of the sugar in a bowl to extract the oils from the zest. Add the lime and sugar mixture to the kola nuts along with the cooled caramel syrup, lime juice, vanilla extract and the remaining sugar, stirring until the sugar has dissolved. Simmer for a further 10 minutes, then remove from the heat and leave to cool completely.

Line a sieve with a double layer of clean J-Cloth or muslin and set over an airtight container, then strain the cooled kola mixture through the cloth or muslin. Store the syrup in the fridge for up to a week.

To serve, mix 50ml (2fl oz) of the kola syrup with 330ml (11fl oz) soda water for 2 glasses.

Iced Kenkey

★ A very popular, inexpensive snack and street food sold throughout Ghana. When I first saw this being made, I was astonished – drinking fermented corn dough? I was even more amazed to learn that I was weaned on the stuff. Kenkey has a powerful fermented flavour and I was expecting not to get past the first mouthful, but I was pleasantly surprised. It's a very distinctive taste and not for everyone, but there are ways to refine the very basic recipe of blended kenkey with iced water and evaporated milk to make it more palatable and, dare I say, even delicious!

You can use either Ga (wrapped in corn cob leaves and steamed) or Fante (wrapped in plantain or banana leaves) kenkey, but in my grandma's house it goes without saying that – as it's a Fante household – the latter wins. However, I find that the former has a slightly less-intimidating degree of fermentation for this quick and easy recipe.

→ **TIP** Add evaporated milk for a creamier taste or 1–2 scoops of vanilla ice cream to make a thick shake.

½ **ball** of Ga or Fante kenkey, diced into small chunks (see Tip on page 112)

6 teaspoons demerara sugar

½ **teaspoon** ground nutmeg

½ **teaspoon** ground cinnamon

½ **teaspoon** vanilla extract and 1 vanilla pod, split lengthways and seeds scraped out

600ml (1 pint) milk

4-5 ice cubes

50g (1¾oz) roasted peanuts, crushed (not ground), for sprinkling

Place all the ingredients except the peanuts in a blender and blend until very smooth.

Pour into tall glasses or cups, sprinkle with the peanuts and serve.

★ Think of this medicinal tea as Ghana's equivalent of camomile tea – a zesty, pungent beverage that has a calming effect. I believe it originates from Cameroon, where they roast guinea pepper along with coffee beans and other spices to create a drink called café touba.

SERVES 2

Guinea Pepper & Ginger Tea

2–3 guinea peppers, crushed

2.5cm (1-inch) piece fresh root ginger (unpeeled if organic)

2 cloves

slice of lemon

500ml (18fl oz) boiling water

Put the guinea peppers, ginger, cloves and slice of lemon in a teapot, pour over the hot water and leave to steep for 5 minutes.

Pour into 2 cups to serve.

★ Super-indulgent and super-delicious!

Divine Hot Chocolate

400ml (14fl oz) almond milk

3 tablespoons Divine cocoa powder

1 tablespoon honey

1 teaspoon ground cinnamon

pinch of sea salt

¼ teaspoon cayenne pepper

To garnish (optional)

1 tablespoon evaporated milk

1 teaspoon grated 70% Divine dark chocolate

→ **TIP** *Divine sustainably and ethically farm their chocolate in Ghana so do source their cocoa powder if you can.*

Put all the ingredients, except those to garnish, in a saucepan and whisk together gently over a low heat until hot.

Pour into 2 mugs, then add a swirl of the evaporated milk and top with the grated chocolate, if you fancy.

. . . .

★ A great warming alternative to mulled wine!

Hot Gin Punch

600ml (1 pint) Sobolo (see page 214)

300ml (10fl oz) dry gin

200ml (7fl oz) sweet sherry

grated **zest and juice** of 1 lemon, plus 2 lemons, sliced

150g (5½oz) demerara or other brown sugar

Put all the ingredients in a saucepan and heat gently, stirring, until the sugar has dissolved and the punch is hot.

Ladle into glasses and serve hot.

★ Amazing as it may sound, this gin uses a superfruit as its main ingredient: the famous baobab (*see page 24*). So as well as offering the many health benefits that the baobab fruit provides, the gin has a really smooth, citrusy sweet and peppery taste – basically, a deliciously floral, surefire winner of a summer cocktail maker!

Whitley Neill Baobab Gin & Bitter Lemon

2 ice cubes

25ml (1fl oz/1 shot) Whitley Neill gin

125ml (4fl oz) Nigerian bitter lemon

½ teaspoon brown sugar

lime wedge, to garnish

Put the ice cubes in a tall glass. Add the remaining ingredients, except the lime wedge, and stir well.

Garnish with a lime wedge and serve immediately.

Whitley Neill Baobab Gin & Tonic

ice cubes

25ml (1fl oz/1 shot) Whitley Neill gin

strip of orange zest and juice of
½ orange, plus orange slice to garnish

100ml (3½fl oz) tonic water

Put some ice cubes in a tall glass. Add the remaining ingredients and stir well to infuse.

Garnish with an orange slice and serve immediately.

- -

★ Inspired by the Ghanaian moonshine *akpeteshie*, a home-brewed spirit made by distilling palm wine or sugar-cane juice and traditionally drunk from a calabash, this will definitely help you get the party started!

SERVES 1

Akpeteshie Fizz

12.5ml (½fl oz/½ shot) dry gin

25ml (1fl oz/1 shot) palm wine

1 tablespoon sugar syrup

ice cubes

100ml (3½fl oz) prosecco, chilled

lime wedge or slice, to garnish

Put the gin, palm wine and sugar syrup in a mixing glass and mix together well with ice cubes, or shake with ice cubes in a cocktail shaker.

Pour into a Champagne flute and top up with the prosecco. Garnish with a lime wedge or slice and serve immediately.

8

★ Dips, Sauces & Salsas

Shito
Hot Pepper Sauce

MAKES ABOUT 500G
(1LB 2OZ)

★ This is the famous Ghanaian hot chilli condiment, which can be made in a variety of ways and every household has its own recipe. It goes really well with both fish and meat, and can be served as a side to most dishes. It can also be used for marinating or as a dressing, dip, spread or topping. I eat it with almost everything, but especially love it as a spicy addition to a cheeseboard with other chutneys.

Many of my restaurant customers who are new to Ghanaian cuisine have likened it to the Malaysian condiment sambal belacha, and they're not wrong – they share the same potent smoky flavour that comes from the addition of ground smoked fish or prawns, as well as its rich texture.

Shito can be either coarse and full of body or smooth, and medium – or extra – hot depending on how much chilli you use, and this is how you'll find it labelled on supermarket and African grocers' shelves. This recipe makes a medium-hot version, which is what we sell at the restaurant in Brixton.

→ **TIP** *You'll find dried smoked fish powder in speciality food stores or online.*

500ml (18fl oz) rapeseed oil, or substitute sunflower or vegetable oil, plus extra if required

3 red onions, finely diced

3 garlic cloves, very finely chopped

8 guinea peppers, ground

7.5cm (3-inch) piece fresh root ginger, finely grated (unpeeled if organic)

1 tablespoon chopped thyme or rosemary leaves (optional)

75g (2¾oz) green kpakpo shito chillies, finely diced (with seeds!), or substitute green Scotch Bonnets, if available, or 2 tablespoons dried chilli flakes

5–6 tablespoons tomato purée

100ml (3½oz) good-quality chicken stock

125g (4½oz) chilli powder

50g (1¾oz) dried ground prawn or shrimp powder

50g (1¾oz) crayfish or smoked fish powder

1 teaspoon freshly ground black pepper

1 teaspoon sea salt

Heat a heavy-based saucepan, then add the oil and fry the onions over a medium heat for 2–3 minutes until translucent.

Add the garlic, guinea peppers, ginger, thyme or rosemary (if using) and chillies and fry together for a few minutes.

Stir in the tomato purée and chicken stock until the mixture has formed a thick paste. Then pour in the chilli powder and continue cooking and stirring for a further 10 minutes.

Finally, add the prawn and crayfish powders, then cook over a low heat for 30–40 minutes, stirring almost continuously to prevent the mixture sticking to the pan. The contents should transform from deep red to very dark brown and the oil will rise to the surface when the sauce is ready. Taste and adjust the seasoning if necessary.

You can choose to blend the sauce with a stick blender or leave it unblended for a coarser texture. Leave to cool, then spoon into sterilized jars (see Tip on page 235). There should be plenty of oil on top of the sauce once it's cooked, so make sure there is a layer about 1cm (½ inch) thick in each jar. But if there is not enough, pour in extra oil to cover. Seal the jars and store in the fridge for up to 1 month.

Green Kpakpo Shito Salsa

MAKES 125-130G (4½OZ)

★ When I last visited Ghana and was trying to ascertain the name of the small cherry-sized chilli used for this fresh, green, spicy salsa that was served with my grilled tilapia, everyone I spoke to responded with 'shito'. The same happened when I held up a Scotch Bonnet or, in fact, any chilli. It took a while surveying and questioning different market traders at Kaneshie Market in Accra before I eventually found the specific name of the kpakpo shito for these cherry chillies (see also page 14).

Serve this salsa as an accompaniment to any rice or yam dish.

➜ **TIP** *The finer you chop the ingredients initially, the easier the mixture will be to grind.*

100g (3½oz) green kpakpo shito (cherry) chillies, roughly chopped (or any other hot green chilli, such as green bird's-eye, jalapeño, habanero or Scotch Bonnet)

2 red or white onions, finely diced

2.5cm (1-inch) piece fresh root ginger, grated (unpeeled if organic)

1 garlic clove, very finely chopped

2 tablespoons lemon or lime juice

2 tablespoons extra virgin olive oil

sea salt and coarsely ground black pepper, to taste

Using a mortar and pestle, or a traditional Ghanaian asanka pot if you have one, grind all the ingredients to a very coarse paste. Alternatively, use a blender or food processor and process gently in brief pulses to retain the coarse texture rather than creating a smooth purée.

TO MAKE RED PEPPER SHITO SALSA: substitute hot red chillies for the green chillies and add 4 medium tomatoes, deseeded and diced. To intensify the flavours of the Red Shito Salsa and extend its shelf life, simmer the mixture for 20–25 minutes, then leave to cool and store in an airtight container in the fridge for up to 5 days.

· ·

Shito Mayo

MAKES 350ML (12FL OZ)

★ This spicy mayo is so moreish, you'll wish you had made more! Add an extra tablespoon of shito if you want to put a real kick into it.

2 egg yolks

2 teaspoons cider vinegar

1 tablespoon Shito (Hot Pepper Sauce; see page 228)

1 heaped teaspoon cayenne pepper

300ml (10fl oz) rapeseed oil

pinch of sea salt

freshly ground black pepper, to taste

Place the egg yolks in a bowl. Add the vinegar, shito and cayenne pepper. Use a balloon whisk to whisk until blended. Add a very small amount of oil and whisk until blended. Continue adding and whisking in the oil gradually until the mixture emulsifies and thickens. Alternatively, put the egg yolks, vinegar, shito and cayenne pepper in a blender or food processor and blend to combine. Then, with the machine running, add the oil in a very slow, thin, steady stream. Season with the sea salt and freshly ground black pepper.

Keep in an airtight container in the fridge for up to 3 days.

eft, from top to ottom: Shito (see page 28); Green kpakpo hito Salsa; Shito Mayo.

★ This flavoured butter works really well as a baste for almost any grilled fish, or use to marinate some asparagus tips or sliced courgette before grilling or pan-frying.

Spiced Baobab Butter

125g (4½oz) salted butter at room temperature, cut into chunks

grated **zest** and **juice of** ½ lemon

1 teaspoon ground hot pepper, or substitute cayenne pepper

1 tablespoon baobab powder

½ teaspoon ground cinnamon

pinch of freshly ground black pepper

Place all the ingredients in a bowl and mash together with a fork. Check the seasoning and adjust to taste.

Spoon the butter along one end of a sheet of baking parchment, then roll up into a mini log, twist the ends to seal and chill until firm, so that it's easy to slice and serve.

→ **TIPS** Try enlivening some simple steamed vegetables with a knob of this zesty spiced butter.

Instead of forming into a roll for slicing, serve the butter in a small ramekin with a baked baguette and a side salad.

★ Think Ghanaian guacamole smoothie, but for dipping – nachos, toasted breads, raw veg...Or it can also be used as a salad dressing.

Avocado & Groundnut Dip

2 ripe avocados

juice of ½ lime or lemon, about **1 tablespoon**

2 tablespoons crushed roasted peanuts

½ teaspoon smoked paprika

½ teaspoon ground cinnamon

½ teaspoon cayenne pepper, or to taste

½ small red onion, finely diced

1 tablespoon rapeseed oil or good-quality olive oil

pinch of sea salt, or to taste

pinch of freshly ground black pepper, or to taste

1–2 tablespoons water

TO GARNISH (AS DESIRED)

chopped coriander or chives

finely chopped red chilli

chopped pistachio nuts

Using a cook's knife, cut each avocado in half lengthways, then slightly twist the halves to separate them. Holding the avocado half containing the stone firmly and carefully on a chopping board, chop the heel of the knife into the stone and lift it out. Cut through the flesh of each half into cubes, then turn the skin inside out and gently scoop the cubed flesh into a blender or food processor.

Add all the remaining ingredients to the blender or food processor and blend to your desired consistency.

Serve garnished with chopped coriander or chives, chilli and/or chopped pistachio nuts, as you like. That's it!

★ This is a great addition to cooked breakfasts, burgers or grilled meats – a spicy, herby relish.

Jollof Relish
Zoe's Ghana Ketchup

500g-750g (1lb 2oz-1lb 10oz) heritage tomatoes or baby plum tomatoes

about 125ml (4fl oz) rapeseed oil

2 small red onions, sliced

1 teaspoon sea salt, plus extra as required

250ml (9fl oz) Jollof Sauce (see page 248)

200-225ml (7-8fl oz) red wine vinegar

150g (5½oz) brown sugar

juice of ½ lime

dash of Worcestershire sauce

Blanch the tomatoes for 30 seconds in a saucepan of boiling water. Using a slotted spoon, transfer to a bowl of iced water. Once cooled, drain the tomatoes, peel, cut in half and chop coarsely.

Heat enough oil in a heavy-based saucepan to cover the base of the pan, add the onions and sauté over a medium heat until soft.

Add the tomatoes and sea salt, cover and cook for 10 minutes.

Add the jollof sauce and cook for a further 5–10 minutes before adding the remaining ingredients. Leave to simmer for 45 minutes–1 hour until reduced and thick. Taste for seasoning and add extra salt if required.

Serve warm, or leave to cool and store in an airtight container in the fridge for later. The relish will keep, refrigerated, for up to 3 months.

★ I LOVE cheese! Our fridge at home is always bursting with different cheeses and there is nothing better with cheese than a good chutney. This festive recipe is a great way to spice up a cheeseboard at Christmas – or all year round in fact – and makes a perfect stocking filler!

MAKES

850G (1LB 14OZ)

Spicy Cranberry Butternut Squash Chutney

2 tablespoons coconut oil

1 star anise

3–5 guinea peppers, crushed, or tropical mixed peppercorns

1 teaspoon dried chilli flakes

5cm (2-inch) piece fresh root ginger, peeled and grated

1 red onion, finely diced

700g (1lb 9oz) butternut squash, peeled, deseeded and cut into 5mm (¼-inch) cubes

250g (9oz) fresh cranberries

175ml (6fl oz) cider vinegar

180–200g (6–7oz) soft light brown sugar

3 whole cloves

→ **TIPS** *You should be able to get at least 4 small jars out of this recipe to make Christmas stocking fillers for friends and family.*

To sterilize jars, wash the jars, then rinse well with hot water, drain and stand in a roasting tin. Warm in a preheated oven, 160°C (325°F), Gas Mark 3, for 10 minutes. Alternatively, wash them in a dishwasher and use as soon as the programme has finished while still warm, but dry.

Heat the oil in a nonstick saucepan until melted, add the star anise, guinea peppers, chilli flakes, ginger and onion and cook together over a medium heat, stirring, until the onion is slightly softened and lightly browned. Set aside.

Mix the squash, cranberries, vinegar, sugar and cloves together in a large flameproof casserole dish and bring to the boil, then stir in the onion and spice mixture.

Turn the heat down and simmer, covered, for about 1½ hours. Alternatively, place in an oven preheated to 150–160°C (300–325°F), Gas Mark 2–3, for up to 2 hours. Keep on eye on it regularly to make sure it's not catching on the pan.

Leave to cool, then spoon into sterilized jars (see Tip, left), seal and store in the fridge for up to 1 month.

Spiced Plantain Chutney

MAKES APPROX. 1KG

(2LB 4OZ) APPROX. 5–6 SMALL JARS

★ Full of intense flavour, this chutney is yet another great way to use slightly overripe plantains (*see also 5 Ways with Plantain, pages* 40–7). Serve as an accompaniment to Jollof (One-pot Rice; *see page* 142) and Kontomire Froe (*see recipe on page* 130 but using goat meat in place of beef), or use as a cheeseboard chutney. You can increase or decrease the spice level to suit your palate.

6 overripe plantains

250ml (9fl oz) malt vinegar or cider vinegar

150g (5½oz) soft dark brown sugar

70g (2½oz) sultanas (optional)

1 tablespoon Kelewele Dry Spice Mix (see page 245)

1 teaspoon dried chilli flakes

1 Scotch Bonnet chilli, deseeded and diced (optional)

2.5cm (1-inch) piece fresh root ginger, grated (unpeeled if organic)

1 tablespoon sea salt

Peel and slice the plantains into 1–2cm (½–¾-inch) chunks.

Combine the plantain pieces with the vinegar and sugar in a heavy-based saucepan and cook over a medium-high heat, stirring regularly to avoid it sticking to the pan, adding water as necessary to prevent it catching (about 250ml, 9fl oz), for 25–30 minutes until the plantain starts to break down and becomes pulpy and most of the liquid has gone.

Stir in all the remaining ingredients and cook for a further 15–20 minutes.

Leave to cool, then transfer to an airtight container and store in the fridge for up to 3 days.

★ Okay, this chutney isn't strictly Ghanaian, but it does use some fantastic Ghanaian ingredients. It's great on a cheeseboard or served on lightly toasted hard dough bread alongside a salad.

MAKES 500G
(1LB 2OZ) APPROX. 3–4 SMALL JARS

Pineapple & Ginger Chutney

1 teaspoon rapeseed oil or olive oil

1 red onion, finely chopped

1 garlic clove, crushed

1 pineapple, peeled, cored and chopped into small chunks

1 Scotch Bonnet chilli, deseeded and finely diced

5cm (2-inch) piece fresh root ginger, grated (unpeeled if organic)

150ml (5fl oz) fresh orange juice

1 tablespoon cider vinegar

250g (9oz) soft light brown sugar

1 teaspoon sea salt

Heat the oil in a small nonstick saucepan, add the onion and garlic and sauté over a medium heat for 5 minutes until soft.

Stir in all the remaining ingredients and simmer for 1 hour until the pineapple has become pulpy and most of the liquid has gone.

Leave to cool, then transfer to an airtight container and store in the fridge for up to 3 days.

→ *Pictured overleaf, from left to right: Spicy Cranberry Butternut Squash Chutney (see page 235); Pineapple & Ginger Chutney (see above); Spiced Plantain Chutney (see left).*

GHANA GO HOME:
A Soundtrack to Eat to

★ Music has always been important in my life – my Dad's phenomenal record collection and ridiculously large base bins featured heavily in my adolescence as part of my education into adulthood. He had an extremely diverse collection ranging from ska and reggae, Motown classics and Detroit doo wop to Fleetwood Mac.

Strangely, apart from a handful of Femi Kuti and High-life pioneers of the 1960s and 1970s – such as the African Brothers Band, King Bruce & the Black Beats and E T Mensah – his Ghanaian section was surprisingly small.

It's not until I started the Ghana Kitchen supper clubs – looking to recreate the atmosphere of Ghana in my living room – that I delved further in to the rich and evocative sounds of High-life and Afro-beat. That was where the Zoe's Ghana Kitchen playlist was born, with 30 or so simple tracks to last the length of a supper club on repeat; it has since grown over time to more than 200 tracks. Now a collaborative process, Zoe's Ghana Kitchen playlist is available to subscribe to and then add to on Spotify.

I've hand-selected these tracks to recreate the atmosphere of those early supper clubs – mixing classics from the 1960s and 1970s with Ghana's ever-growing and increasingly mainstream Afro-beat sounds.

Eat your way through this playlist and then burn off the calories by dancing afterwards!

	Artist	Track	Album	Song Length
1	Jay Ghartey, Sarkodie	*My Lady*	Hiplife Mix	4:13
2	Sarkodie	*You Go Kill Me (feat. El)*	(single)	3:45
3	Femi Kuti	*1,2,3,4*	Africa Shrine	4:31
4	Samini	*Sweet Girls (feat. Nameless)*	Dagaati	4:32
5	Tinny	*Obi Do Ba*	Makola Kwakwe	6:03
6	Ghana M'Baye	*N'Diakhass*	Baye Falle Djembe	4:24
7	Guru, Dr Cryme	*Ooh My God (feat. Dr Cryme & Guru)*	Pressure	4:08
8	Ruff-N-Smooth	*Swagger*	Life Is Rough & Smooth	4:43

	Artist	Track	Album	Song Length
9	Femi Kuti	*Yeparipa*	Africa For Africa	3:33
10	Eric Agyeman	*Ao Me Wiasei Mu*	Ghana Gold	5:10
11	4x4	*Waist and Power (African Man)*	(single)	5:05
12	Sarkodie	*Fair Warning Aka Tema Part 2*	(single)	5:55
13	Black Rasta	*Cocaine In The Palace (feat. Mugeez)*	Naked Wire	4:57
14	Hot Chip, William Onyeabor	*Atomic Bomb - Cover*	What?!	7:16
15	Tic Tac	*Fefe Na Efe*	Fefe Ma Efe	5:54
16	Akon	*Be With You*	Freedom (int'l version)	3:51
17	Eazzy	*Wengeze*	(single)	3:37
18	Ghana Gospel Music	*The Pillar Of My Life*	Volume 1	4:44
19	E T Mensah, The Tempos	*Afi Fro Fro*	All For You	2:34
20	Sarkodie	*Obobi*	Obobi Signle	2:18
21	Jay Ghartey, Okyeame Kwame	*Me Do Wo (feat. Okyeame Kwame)*	Me Do Wo	4:09
22	D'banj	*Fall In Love*	51 Lex Presents If Dey Crase	4:14
23	African Brothers	*Self Reliance*	Soundway presents Ghana Soundz (Afro-beat, Funl and Fusion in 1970s Ghana)	8:33
24	D'banj	*Mr Endowed*	Safari	4:16
25	Wande Coal feat. D'Banj	*You Bad*	51 Lex Records Presents Carnizelas Vol 2	4:08
26	P-Square	*Do Me*	Game Over	4:43
27	Ghana High-life and Other	*Bus Conductor*	Ghana High-life and Other	2:23
28	P-Square	*Roll It*	Game Over	4:17
29	Rob	*Make It Fast, Make It Slow*	Soundway presents Ghana Soundz (Afro-Beat, Funl and Fusion in 1970s Ghana)	5:25
30	Cutlass Dance Band	Kofi Wedzidzi	Ghana Funk	3:15
31	Pidgen Allstars	*Toto Mechanic (feat. Kwaku-T remix)*	Black Stars – Ghana's Hiplife Generation	4:04
32	William Onyeabor	Body and Soul	World Psychedelic Classic 5: Who Is William Onyeabor?	10:08
33	Apagya Show Band	*Kwaakwa*	Ghana Funk	3:52
34	FBS Crew	*Oldman Boogey*	Black Stars – Ghana's Hiplife Generation	5:33
35	E T Mensah	*Kaa No Wa*	Day By Day	3:38
36	Policy	*Something You Will Never Forget*	What?!	5:36
37	Nkasei	*Edua Neb U (feat. Reggie Rockstone)*	Black Stars – Ghana's Hiplife Generation	6:04
38	Ghana M'Baye	*Bakk*	Baye Falle Djembe	4:05
39	Daphni	*Ye Ye- Re Work*	What?!	6:04
40	C K Mann	*Okuan Tsentsen Awar*	Ghana Funk	6:44

SPICE MIXES

Here are some great spice mixes you can prepare and store in the cupboard to have on hand for marinades and to speed up cooking times when it comes to making the dishes in the book.

Ghanaian Five-spice Mix

★ This is a great fragrant spice mix for use in baking, especially during the festive season. Simply make up a batch and add one or two teaspoons to biscuit dough or spiced cake or bread recipes.

MAKES A GENEROUS 5½ TABLESPOONS

4 tablespoons ground cubeb pepper

1 teaspoon ground or freshly grated nutmeg

2 teaspoons ground cloves

1 teaspoon ground cinnamon

1 teaspoon ground ginger

Mix all the ingredients together in a bowl. Store in an airtight container in a cool, dark place and use within a few months.

Jollof Dry Spice Mix

★ This is a great secret weapon to bring out for marinating meat before grilling, frying, baking or barbecuing. It works particularly well with chicken (*see Jollof Spiced Chicken Skewers and Jollof Fried Chicken, pages 151 and 138*) and fish, and you can also add it when you're making Jollof Sauce and Jollof (One-pot Rice; *see pages 248 and 142*).

MAKES ABOUT 190G (6½OZ)

25g (1oz) ground ginger

25g (1oz) garlic powder

20g (¾oz) dried chilli flakes

35g (1¼oz) dried thyme

25g (1oz) ground cinnamon

20g (¾oz) ground ginger

15g (½oz) ground nutmeg

15g (½oz) ground coriander

¼ teaspoon cooking salt

¼ teaspoon freshly ground black pepper

scant 1 teaspoon dried ground prawn/shrimp or crayfish powder (optional)

Mix all the ingredients together in a bowl. Store in an airtight container in a cool, dark place and use within a few months.

Kelewele Dry Spice Mix

★ This is a spice mix for Kelewele – a simple, quick side dish of spiced and fried plantain (*see page 44*), a common street-food snack throughout Ghana. It's a good one to keep in the cupboard, as it can also be used to make Spiced Plantain Chutney (*see page 236*), or in baking.

MAKES ABOUT 5½ TABLESPOONS

2 tablespoons ground ginger

1 tablespoon ground cinnamon

1 tablespoon ground or freshly grated nutmeg

1 tablespoon cayenne pepper

½ tablespoon ground cloves

Mix all the ingredients together in a bowl. Store in an airtight container in a cool, dark place and use within a few months.

African Peppered Steak Spice Mix

★ Use from 1 teaspoon to 1 tablespoon mixed with 1 tablespoon olive oil to season beef or venison steaks before grilling. As with all marinades, the longer the meat is left to marinate the better, so ideally leave it overnight, but aim for at least 1–2 hours.

MAKES ABOUT 100G (3½OZ)

50g (1¾oz) grains of paradise

30g (1oz) ground cubeb pepper

1 teaspoon ground hot pepper, or substitute cayenne pepper

1 teaspoon sea salt

1 tablespoon dried rosemary (optional)

Using a mortar and pestle, crush the grains of paradise and then blend with the other ingredients.

Store in an airtight container in a cool, dark place and use within a few months.

★ Suya is the king of spice rubs in Ghana, the flavouring of choice for the hugely popular street-food style of cooking on open charcoal grills. You can use this mix to marinate any meat or seafood of your choice before barbecuing or grilling. In Ghana, it's most commonly used for chargrilled chicken, beef, goat and prawn kebabs.

MAKES ABOUT 180–230G (6¼–8¼OZ)

Suya Spice Rub

150–200g (5½–7oz) ground roasted peanuts, or smooth peanut butter

2 teaspoons ground hot pepper, or substitute cayenne pepper

½ teaspoon smoked paprika

1 teaspoon ground ginger

1 teaspoon ground nutmeg

1 teaspoon garlic powder

½ teaspoon ground cloves

½ teaspoon ground cinnamon

1 teaspoon sea salt

ADDITIONAL FRESH SEASONINGS (OPTIONAL)

2 tablespoons groundnut oil (sunflower oil will do)

3 garlic cloves, very finely chopped or grated

5cm (2-inch) piece fresh root ginger, grated (unpeeled if organic)

sprig of thyme, leaves picked

1 tablespoon lime juice (optional)

Mix all the ingredients for the dry spice mix together in a bowl. Store in an airtight container in a cool, dark place, or in the fridge if made with peanut butter, and use within a few months.

For up to 500g (1lb 2oz) meat or seafood, use 3–4 tablespoons of the dry spice mix as a rub, or mix with the oil and fresh seasonings in a bowl (the mixture will keep in an airtight container in the fridge for 1–3 days), then rub into the tenderized meat, or seafood (see Tips, below). Cover and leave to marinate in the fridge for at least 1–2 hours, preferably overnight.

→ **TIPS** Simply scale the quantities given above up or down according to how much meat or seafood you are cooking.

To tenderize meat before rubbing with the marinade, gently pound with the back of a wooden spoon on both sides on a chopping board.

SAUCES

Here are some super-easy recipes for sauces that you can cook up in advance and keep on hand to speed up what would otherwise be lengthy cooking times for some of the dishes in the book, leaving you with more time for chatting when you're having guests over for dinner.

Chalé Sauce

★ This basic recipe is based on my dad's everyday cooking sauce. He would whip this up and then literally throw in any type of meat, fish or protein, but it was always tasty.

You can just blend the ingredients and store the uncooked sauce for later use, or cook it and then leave to cool – either way it saves time when making many of the recipes in this book. I make a big batch of this at least once a week – you can easily double the quantity if you want to make a bigger batch, although it's not necessary to increase the Scotch Bonnet unless you like it extra-extra-hot!

MAKES 500ML (18FL OZ)

400g (14oz) can tomatoes or **250g (9oz)** fresh tomatoes

30g (1oz) or 2 tablespoons tomato purée

1 onion, roughly chopped

5cm (2-inch) piece fresh root ginger, grated (unpeeled if organic)

1 red Scotch Bonnet chilli, deseeded

1 tablespoon dried chilli flakes

1 teaspoon sea salt

3 garlic cloves (optional)

TO COOK

1 tablespoon sunflower oil

1 onion, finely diced

1 teaspoon curry powder

1 teaspoon extra-hot chilli powder

Place all the ingredients except the 'to cook' ones in a blender and blend together until you have a fairly smooth paste. This is your uncooked chalé sauce.

For cooked chalé sauce, heat the oil in a heavy-based saucepan, add the onion and sauté over a medium heat for a few minutes until softened. Then add the curry powder and chilli powder and stir thoroughly to coat the onion evenly. Add the blended tomato mixture and simmer gently for 35–40 minutes.

Use straight away, or leave to cool then store in an airtight container in the fridge for up to 3 days, or freeze for future use.

★ This is a bit of a shortcut for speeding up the making of Jollof (One-pot Rice; *see* page 142). It's also a great recipe for forming the basis of a spicy ketchup to accompany rice or yam dishes.

Jollof Sauce

MAKES ABOUT 1 LITRE (1¾ PINTS)

sunflower or other cooking oil

1 large onion, finely diced

½ tablespoon curry powder

½ tablespoon chilli powder

2.5cm (1-inch) piece fresh root ginger, grated (unpeeled if organic)

1 garlic clove, crushed

1 red Scotch Bonnet chilli, deseeded and roughly chopped (optional)

25g (1oz) thyme leaves, chopped (optional)

1 heaped tablespoon Jollof Dry Spice Mix (see page 244)

400g (14fl oz) can tomatoes or **250g (9oz)** fresh tomatoes, diced

1 heaped tablespoon tomato purée

1 teaspoon sea salt, or more to taste

100ml (3½fl oz) good-quality chicken or vegetable stock

Heat enough sunflower or other cooking oil to cover the base of a heavy-based saucepan, add the onion and sauté over a medium heat until translucent. Stir in the curry powder and chilli powder and gently fry for a further 2 minutes.

Add the ginger, garlic, Scotch Bonnet, thyme (if using) and jollof dry spice mix and stir well. Then add the tomatoes and tomato purée, sea salt and stock and stir once more before blending thoroughly with a stick blender until smooth.

Simmer over a medium–low heat for 30–40 minutes (closer to 40 minutes if using canned tomatoes in order to cook out the acidity of the tomatoes). Taste for seasoning and add extra sea salt if required.

Leave to cool and then store in an airtight container in the fridge for up to 3 days, or freeze for future use.

★ My ultimate childhood comfort food – I absolutely love this sauce! And here's a way to fast-forward a few steps to reach the desired result faster.

Peanut Sauce

MAKES 850–900ML (ABOUT 1½ PINTS)

1 tablespoon groundnut oil

1 onion, finely diced

1 tablespoon extra-hot chilli powder

1 tablespoon curry powder

1 garlic clove, crushed

5cm (2-inch) piece fresh root ginger, grated (unpeeled if organic)

1 red Scotch Bonnet chilli, pierced

3 tablespoons crushed roasted peanuts

2 teaspoons sea salt

1 teaspoon freshly ground black pepper

500ml (18fl oz) uncooked Chalé Sauce (see page 247)

500ml (18fl oz) good-quality vegetable stock (you can use chicken or beef stock if adding the sauce to a meat dish)

100–200g (3½–7oz) organic peanut butter, depending on how thick you want the sauce

8 green kpakpo shito (cherry) chillies, or substitute green habanero chillies

Heat the groundnut oil in a heavy-based saucepan, add the onion and sauté over a medium heat for 2 minutes. Stir in the chilli powder and curry powder, then add the garlic, ginger, Scotch Bonnet, crushed peanuts, sea salt and black pepper and stir well – lots of punchy aroma should be rising from the pot at this point.

Stir in the chalé sauce and vegetable stock and bring to the boil, then reduce the heat and simmer for 15–20 minutes.

Add the peanut butter 1 tablespoon at a time, while stirring, until it has all dissolved, then use a stick blender to blend all the ingredients to a smooth consistency.

Add the whole kpakpo shito chillies to the sauce and leave to simmer over a low heat for at least a further 30 minutes before serving, or leave to cool and then store in an airtight container in the fridge for up to 5 days. Alternatively, freeze for future use. You can then simply reheat as much sauce as needed at the time as a side dip, or create a soup by adding diced yams and plantain or cooking meat in the sauce for a more substantial meal.

→ **TIP** I often leave the peanut sauce to simmer for up to 2 hours so that the flavours really infuse, but 30–40 minutes is good enough.

INDEX

SUPPLIERS & STOCKISTS

★ **UK**

Abu Bakar Supermarket,
37 Queens Road,
Leeds
LS6 1NY

Africa Shopping Centre,
24-26 Electric Avenue,
London
SW9 8JR

African Caribbean Food
Store,
342 Soho Road,
Birmingham
B21 9QL

African Crest,
193 Gorgie Road,
Edinburgh
EH11 1TT
www.africancrest.com

African Embassy African
Foods,
293 Duke Street,
Glasgow
G31 1HX
www.africanembassy.
co.uk

African Food Store,
156 Burnt Oak
Broadway,
Edgware,
London
HA8 0AX

Afrik Mart,
4 Preston Road,
North Laine,
Brighton
BN1 4QF

Afrocarib
www.afrocarib.co.uk

Afro-Caribbean
Supermarket,
36 Duke Street,
Chelmsford
CM1 1HY

AfroExpress
www.afroexpress.co

Afro-Mart,
21 Story Street,
Kingston upon Hull
HU1 3SA

B & T African
Supermarket,
105 Far Gosford Street,
Coventry
CV1 5EA

B & Y African Tropical
Foods,
56 Goldhawk Rd,
London
W12 8HA

Bangla Bazar,
175-177 Ormeau Rd,
Belfast
BT7 1SQ

Biltong & Bangers,
161 High St,
Southampton
SO14 2BT
www.
biltongandbangers.com

Biltong Direct,
Woodhall Parade,
4a Woodhall Road,
Chelmsford
CM1 4BA
www.biltongdirect.
co.uk/our-stores

Bims African Food Store,
102 Rye Ln,
London
SE15 4RZ

Brixton Market,
Electric Avenue,
London
SW9 8JX
www.brixtonmarket.net

Canterbury Wholefoods,
1 Iron Bar Ln,
Canterbury
CT1 2HN
www.canterbury-
wholefoods.co.uk

Continental Food Stores,
119 Old Tiverton Rd,
Exeter
EX4 6LD
www.continentalfoods
exeter.com

De Africa,
163 Dalry Road,
Edinburgh
EH11 2EB
www.deafrica.co.uk

Divine Love African
Store,
575 W Derby Rd,
Liverpool
L13 8AE

Exodus Express,
43 Bath St,
Gravesend
DA11 0DE

Franrit African
Supermarket,
218 Beverley Road,
Hull
HU5 1AH

Ghanalinks
www.ghanalinks.co.uk

Global Africa,
78 Hulme High St,
Manchester
M15 5JP

John and Biola Foods,
13 Joyce Dawson Way,
London
SE28 8RA
www.johnandbiola.co.uk

Just Here Afri Foods,
235a, Staveley Rd,
Wolverhampton
WV1 4RH

JWDKS African Food,
41 West St,
St. Philips,
Bristol
BS2 0BZ

Mama African Food,
126 West Road,
Newcastle Upon Tyne
NE4 9QA

Medina Continental
Foodstore,
79-83 Radford Road,
Nottingham
NG7 5DR

Moston Superstore,
7 Pym Street,
Manchester
M40 9WE

Olaiya African Food
Store Ltd,
Chipperfield Road,
Orpington
BR5 2LJ

Olumo Foods
www.olumofoods.co.uk

Osas African Food Shop,
263 Westgate Road,
Newcastle upon Tyne
NE4 6AH
www.
osasafricanfoodshop.
co.uk

Ridley Road Market,
51 - 63 Ridley Rd,
Dalston,
London
E8 2NP
www.ridleyroad.co.uk

S J Supermarket,
267 Anlaby Road,
Hull
HU3 2SE

Sami African Foods,
325 Moston Lane,
Moston,
Manchester
M40 9NL

Savanna,
Victoria Station,
London
SW1V 1JT
www.thesavanna.co.uk

Sollys African Village,
381-383 Great Western
Road,
Glasgow
G4 9HY
www.sollysafricanvillage.
co.uk

Stella's Groceries and
Vegetables,
154 Rye Lane,
Peckham,
London
SE15 4NB

Top Food Centre,
4-6 Upper Clapton
Road,
Lower Clapton,
London
E5 8AE

Vicky's African &
Caribbean Food Store,
78 Hartley Road,
Nottingham
G7 3AF

Wiloks International
Food Store,
217/219 Radford Rd,
Nottingham
NG7 5GT
www.wiloksinternational.
co.uk

Yabo African Foods,
Shepherds Bush Market,
London
W12 8DE

Xquisite Africa,
148 City Rd,
Cardiff
CF24 3DR
www.xquisiteafrica.
co.uk/xafrica

★ **A special shout out to
my so, so solid suppliers
in Ridley Road, Dalston
and Brixton – all excellent
markets for a plethora
of african foodstuffs but
I have to highlight the
following traders:**

A.B. Tropical Foods,
Kaneshie Market,
212 Ridley Road,
Dalston,
London
E8 2NH
*Good range of hard-to-
find spices, pulses and
leaves.*

Kumasi Market,
3rd Avenue,
27-28 Brixton Village,
London
SW9 8PR
*Don't expect too much
eye contact but they
have EVERYTHING.*

Kwaso Trading,
204 Ridley Road,
Dalston,
London
E8 2NH
Super friendly.

London Drinks Co
www.london-drinks.
co.uk
*Specialty Ghanaian
beers and soft drinks.*

Madina Store,
78 Kingsland High street,
Dalston,
London
E8 2NS
*Saj and his family at
Madina have been
doing me a solid for
years! I love them.*

The Vintage Grocery
Store,
186 Ridley Road,
Dalston,
London
E8 2NH
*Sef and his aunt stock
the best Fante kenkey,
among other Ghanaian
treats.*

★ Europe

Abyssinia African
Grocery,
Jan Pieter Heijestraat
186,
1054 MN Amsterdam,
Netherlands
www.abyssiniagrocery.nl

Africa Musso,
21 Grande Rue de la
Guillotière,
69007 Lyon,
France

Africa Store,
65 Grande Rue de la
Guillotière,
69007 Lyon,
France

Afro-Karibik Markt,
Grunerstraße 5,
10179 Berlin,
Germany

Alpha and Omega
International Afro Shop,
Weserstraße 3,
12047 Berlin,
Germany
www.alphaandomega
afroshop.com

Epicerie Ivoirienne,
34 Rue des Poissonniers,
75018 Paris,
France

Ghana House,
Kölner Str. 43A,
40211 Düsseldorf,
Germany
www.ghanahouse.de

MAS Impex (Asian
und Afro Lebensmittel
Supermarkt),
Wilstorfer Street 49,
21073 Hamburg,
Germany
www.masimpex.com

Max Afro Shop,
Karl-Marx-Straße 25,
12043 Berlin,
Germany
maxafroshop.blogspot.
co.uk

Remon Afro Asian
Market,
West-Kruiskade 87,
3014AN Rotterdam,
Netherlands

World Wide Food TN. e.K.,
Stuvkamp 24,
22081 Hamburg,
Germany
www.worldwidefood.de

★ Sustainable stockists

Aduna
*Working with famers
in Ghana to create
sustainable moringa,
baobab and cocoa
health foods.*
www.aduna.com/
collections/all

Caratino
*Working to produce
sustainable palm oil
and derivatives.*
www.carotino.co.uk

Coconut Merchant
*Ethically sourced
coconut oil and related
products.*
www.coconut-merchant.
com

Divine Chocolate
*Working with famers
in Ghana to create
sustainable farming
methods in cocoa
production.*
www.divinechocolate.
com

*A few brands putting
top quality peanut
butter to market:*
- Meridian Foods
www.meridianfoods.
co.uk

- Pics Peanut Butter
www.picspeanutbutter.
com

- Whole Earth Foods
www.wholeearthfoods.
com

**All details correct at
time of printing.**

UK/US GLOSSARY

UK	=	US
aubergine	=	eggplant
baking sheet	=	cookie sheet
baking tin or tray	=	baking pan
bavette steak	=	flank steak
black pudding	=	blood sausage
cake mixture	=	batter
cake tin	=	cake pan
caster sugar	=	superfine sugar
chicken breast strips	=	chicken tenders
clingfilm	=	plastic wrap
coriander (fresh)	=	cilantro
coriander (spice)	=	coriander
cornflour	=	cornstarch
courgette	=	zucchini
demerara sugar	=	light brown raw cane sugar from Guyana
fishmonger	=	fish dealer
flameproof casserole dish	=	Dutch oven
greaseproof paper	=	nonstick parchment paper
griddle pan	=	ridged grill pan
grill	=	broiler
groundnuts	=	peanuts
groundnut oil	=	peanut oil

UK	=	US
heritage tomatoes	=	heirloom tomatoes
icing sugar	=	confectioners' sugar
king prawn or tiger prawn	=	jumbo shrimp
kitchen paper	=	paper towels
loaf tin	=	loaf pan
minced lamb, beef, pork, etc.	=	ground lamb, ground beef, ground pork
muslin	=	cheesecloth
natural yogurt	=	plain yogurt
plain flour	=	all-purpose flour
prawn	=	shrimp
pudding rice	=	short-grain rice, such as Arborio
rapeseed oil	=	canola oil
rocket	=	arugula
rump tail (beef)	=	tri tip
shop-bought	=	ready-made
spring greens	=	collard greens
spring onions	=	scallions
starter	=	appetizer
sultana	=	golden raisin
tomato purée	=	tomato paste
vanilla pod	=	vanilla bean

COOKERY NOTES

Standard level spoon measurements are used in all recipes. 1 tablespoon = one 15ml spoon; 1 teaspoon = one 5ml spoon.

Eggs should be medium, free-range, unless otherwise stated. The Department of Health advises that eggs should not be consumed raw. This book contains dishes made with raw or lightly cooked eggs. It is prudent for more vulnerable people such as pregnant and nursing mothers, invalids, the elderly, babies and young children to avoid uncooked or lightly cooked dishes made with eggs. Once prepared these dishes should be kept refrigerated and used promptly.

Ovens should be preheated to the specific temperature – if using a fan-assisted oven, follow manufacturer's instructions for adjusting the time and the temperature.

This book includes dishes made with nuts and nut derivatives. It is advisable for those with known allergic reactions to nuts and nut derivatives and those who may be potentially vulnerable to these allergies, such as pregnant and nursing mothers, invalids, the elderly, babies and children, to avoid dishes made with nuts and nut oils. It is also prudent to check the labels of pre-prepared ingredients for the possible inclusion of nut derivatives.

To sterilize jars, wash the jars, then rinse well with hot water, drain and stand in a roasting tin. Warm in a preheated oven, 160°C (325°F), Gas Mark 3, for 10 minutes. Alternatively, wash them in a dishwasher and use as soon as the programme has finished while still warm, but dry.

ACKNOWLEDGEMENTS

Six years ago, during Hackney Wicked, I made a huge pot of my favourite childhood dish – Peanut Butter Soup and Fried Plantain. People came to eat and socialize in droves. Since that day, I have had the support and encouragement of far too many people to mention here that have taken me on an incredible food journey. Thank you all but especially…

Leanne Medley – thank you for your steadfast support, encouragement and daily inspirations that push me every day to challenge myself.

Jasmine Johnson – thank you for steering me toward a more creative life. Without your help and influence Zoe's Ghana Kitchen might not have been born.

Yassa Khan – for all your creative direction, inspiration, support and hand-holding in the early years.

My sister Natalie Adjonyoh – constant champion and supporter of everything I do and pillar on which I constantly lean.

Francis Spufford at Goldsmith's University – for adamantly encouraging me to both write and cook and that both would feed each other.

Special thanks to: Elise Dillsworth for helping to get this book published; The Cultural Group CIC for spell-checking my Fante; Akua Afram (DJ Aries) for submitting a playlist; Laurel Sills for being a willing copy editor; Cat Drew for the lovely map of Ghana.

A thousand thanks to all our customers at Zoe's Ghana Kitchen in Brixton, to all those who have ever been to one of my supper clubs or pop ups and to a very long list of supporters and encouragers along the way that include but are not limited to: Dan Ainsworth; Ahmad Al Masri; Rosie Tonkin; Laura Kaye; Aleksandra Kielpinska; Jeffrey Lennon; David Coles and the team at Kick Start Ghana; Odira Morewabone; Sven Muenden; Bisi Oyekanmi; Amy Goodhall; Dani Berg; Chris Hurrell; Gracie Thornton; Ruth Holland; Esther Suave (formerly of Tip Berlin) for making Berlin events and supper clubs a possibility through your wonderful review.

And, of course, to my Dad (and his Chalé sauce) for bringing home ingredients that made me inquisitive about Ghanaian food, and to Mum for keeping up with a Ghanaian diet even when he wasn't around.

Lastly, thanks to all my followers on Instagram and Twitter @ghanakitchen and @zoeadjonyoh

Mwah!

X

PICTURE CREDITS

Page 7: left and centre, Copyright © Zoe's Ghana Kitchen Ltd; top right, Copyright © Claire Tang; bottom right, Copyright © Chris Coulson © cwiss. Page 10: map Copyright © Cat Drew www.cargocollective.com/catdrew.